The 'Victorian Day' series sets out not only to teach history but to bring it to life by tracing the daily routine of a typical individual from the time he got up in the morning until he went to bed at night. A regular and ordered day in the life of a Victorian 'peeler' would be far from typical, however, and this story takes place mainly in the hours of night and the early morning.

The 'hero' of the story is Arnold Pipkin, a policeman stationed at Bow Street whose beat is on the edge of the infamous rookeries of St Giles. The date is 14 July 1850, just twenty-one years after the police force was founded. In the course of his day's, or night's, work he helps to cope with a fire and an escaped prisoner, but his main obstacle is the ferocious poverty he meets on all sides among the people of St Giles.

A final chapter gives a detailed survey of the growth of the organised police force, and the consequent social changes in the attitudes to crime in Victorian England. This is followed by a section of ideas and suggestions for further work and a guide to some of the available sources. These draw together the wealth of documentation and historical description contained in the 'story' section, and help to make the book extremely useful to teachers and students of Victorian and social history, and especially those involved in projects and follow-up work for examinations such as CSE.

UNWIN VICTORIAN DAY SERIES: 3

A Day in the Life of a Victorian Policeman

UNWIN VICTORIAN DAY SERIES

Series Editor: Frank E. Huggett

A Day in the Life of
A VICTORIAN
POLICEMAN

JOHN GARFORTH

LONDON · GEORGE ALLEN & UNWIN LTD
Ruskin House   Museum Street

ISBN 0 04 942122 0 Cloth
      0 04 942123 9 Paper

Filmset in 12 on 13 point Baskerville and printed
Offset Litho in Great Britain by Cox & Wyman Ltd
London, Fakenham and Reading

Contents

Illustrations

Acknowledgements

Figures 3, 5, 6, 9 and 11 are reproduced by kind permission of Westminster Public Libraries; Figures 2, 7, 16, 18, 20 and 31 by kind permission of Haringey Public Libraries; and Figures 12, 22, 23, 25, 27 and 28 by kind permission of the Metropolitan Police, New Scotland Yard. We should also like to acknowledge the assistance of Mr. F. Jeapes and Mr. E. Jukes in the preparation of these illustrations.

Preface

This book reconstructs one day, Thursday, 4 July 1850, in the life of a policeman; it is the story of Arnold Pipkin.

No Victorian 'peeler' has left a written record of his daily life, and even the traditional policeman's notebook was not used as the regular diary we would now expect. But details of how they lived are easy to reconstruct from contemporary sources, and the situation they had to contend with is well documented.

For a Victorian policeman one day was much the same as another—it was dull, routine plodding with highly dramatic interruptions. Each day there was the parade and the pep talk, walking the beat from nine till six at night, and each day there were arrests and fights and fires and deaths and crimes, there were mornings in court and afternoons at home in bed. It was a dull routine amid the continuing melodrama of poverty and lawlessness. The 'peeler' on the beat saw all the activity but he had none of the explanations, he seldom knew why or discovered what happened next.

In 1850 the police force came of age, Sir Robert Peel died and Colonel Rowan retired, Henry Mayhew was collecting his invaluable sketches of London life and Dickens was editing a magazine called *Household Words*. The Victorian age was at its most self-confident, about to celebrate the virtues of high mindedness and the industrial revolution with the Great Exhibition. Yet life was grim for a vast number of people.

Most of this book consists of a simple narrative and a descriptive account of Arnold Pipkin's day, which is suitable for individual study or reading in class. It is profusely illustrated with photographs, which not only bring the story alive but should also stimulate an interest in the period and its problems. Many parts of the text can be used as a starting point for local investigations, and some further suggestions are contained in Appendix 2.

Whilst it can be argued that a policeman's view of society is somewhat distorted, with its emphasis on crime, poverty and violence, it is likely that the distortion offers a sharply corrective insight into the nature of that society. However, Arnold Pipkin's viewpoint has to be set in the wider national context. It must be remembered that it was only the Metropolitan police force which came into existence in 1829; the rest of the country followed slowly, and developments were related to such factors as prison reform, political and social emancipation, industrial conditions, and these are dealt with at some length in the final chapter, 'The National Scene'. This is more suitable for study by the whole class under the teacher's guidance.

Controlling the theatre crowds was a necessary part of a 'peeler's' evening duty

1. *NIGHT—ON THE BEAT*

The clock on St Giles' Church struck twelve as Arnold Pipkin resumed his beat. He felt better now. There was nothing like a tankard of stout to help a policeman through the long night. He tucked his fingers into his belt and walked away. The streets were quiet tonight—much too quiet. Arnold paused at the end of Little Earl Street and listened. There had been no fights, and even the drunks were now going home in silence.

It was the kind of night when it was easy to imagine that a hundred pairs of eyes were watching from behind broken doorways and rickety gates. Arnold stopped whistling; it sounded so loud. He wished his boots were not so heavy. He sensed a movement in the shadows of Monmouth Court. He crossed the cobbled street to investigate, casually, at the regulation two and a half miles an hour, with his right hand tucked under the swallow tail of his coat where his truncheon was kept. He wished there was a little more moonlight.

'Hullo,' he called gruffly.

No answer. Whatever it was scurried deeper into the blackness.

'Hey, you there!'

Arnold shone his bullseye lantern into the dingy alleyway. It was probably nothing, but he was poised ready to move smartly on in case it were something dangerous. He was not feeling heroic this evening. But then he relaxed. He could just distinguish a female figure huddled against the gates of Jemmy Catnach's printing works.

'I can see you, young Amy!'

Amy Hill emerged from the shadows with a timid smile. 'Hello, Mr Pipkin,' she said nervously. 'I didn't know it was you on your rounds.' In the flickering light of the bullseye lantern Amy looked quite pretty; she was sixteen, and the flurry of ribbons, artificial flowers and bright colours was very attractive. In the daylight her face was already lined by the hardships of her life.

'Why are you hiding in doorways, Amy?' he asked, with an attempt at severity. 'Did you think I might creep up behind and rob you?'

'Bless you, no, Mr Pipkin,' she said with a laugh. 'But I was nervous. There's such a strange feeling in the Holy Land tonight. . . .'

The Holy Land was the local name for the district beyond Arnold's beat; it was a slum area that no policeman cared to enter. Arnold put his arm round the girl's thin shoulders and led her back into the gaslit safety of Seven Dials. To Arnold's mind the real tragedy of the Holy Land was that young girls like Amy lived there. It was no place for bringing up children.

'Has Jake Sweeting turned up yet, Amy?'

She hunched her shoulders. 'Jake Sweeting?'

'Jake Sweeting,' he repeated. 'Jake escaped from Cold Bath Fields prison yesterday afternoon. He'll be here in the Holy Land pretty soon.'

She shook her head. 'I wouldn't know anything about that, Mr Pipkin.'

Arnold sighed. 'Go home, Amy,' he said. 'Tell Mrs Goddard I'll be there as usual at three o'clock.'

Amy hurried silently away along Earlham Street and vanished into the Holy Land. Poor kid. Although, in fact, Amy could be a regular wildcat, with an ability to swear that would surprise even a costermonger. But she was always pleasant to Arnold. He told himself that he brought out the best in people.

He continued round his beat. Number four beat of Section One, E Division, along both sides of Little St Andrew Street from Seven Dials to West Street, with the side of West Street and both sides of Little Earl Street, back to the Seven Dials, including Tower Street, Lumber Court and Monmouth Court. He was supposed to go round in fourteen minutes. It was like a goldfish bowl;

The Seven Dials in 1850, with Little Earl Street on the left

Arnold sometimes imagined he could see his own tail disappearing in the distance as he turned the corner.

Crunch, crunch, crunch, along West Street. He felt slightly easier as he left the Holy Land behind and made for the fringe of Covent Garden market. The porters were noisy and busy and earning an honest living. They sold half their fruit and vegetables to costers and street traders, who needed watching. But Arnold felt safer tonight among men who had a job to do.

'Watch it, Fred, here's an esclop,' somebody called. Esclop was backslang for police. Occasionally a strange coster would treat Arnold as an intruder, a symbol of authority, but he was soon put in his place by the others. 'That's not an esclop, that's our Arnold!' The costers were colourful figures in their long velvet jackets, cord trousers gathered at the knees and elaborately stitched boots. So long as you didn't trust them, as Arnold frequently said, they were harmless.

He stopped to allow a cartload of apples past. The horse looked tired from its six-hour journey through Kent or Surrey; the driver cracked his whip and shouted 'Careep, there!' which seemed to mean turn right and head for Joe Salmon's yard.

The problem of congestion in Covent Garden was a continuous cause of trouble. People felt that Arnold should keep the highways clear of flower stalls, and that he should keep the traffic moving. But what could he do about it? There were simply too many people, and too many carriages. This was, after all, 1850.

A hundred years ago the area had been inhabited by wealthy people, and they had drawn up a petition to the Duke of Bedford about the decline of the district. But the Garden had continued to decline—it had become a vast, sprawling market and a haunt of the underworld. In 1813 an Act had been passed by Parliament to regulate the market, but that Act had been repealed ten years later. Then a new covered market had been built to accommodate all the traders. With the new covered market more traders had flocked into the area, and the sprawl outwards had continued. It was like the traffic problem. Ever since they had built New Oxford Street through the northern end of St Giles the extra traffic had caused more congestion than before.

In addition to the traders and the paupers there were now swarms of tourists to add to the problem; rich young men gathered to mock the porters at work or to marvel at the sight of nine or ten baskets balanced on a porter's head; gentlemen came to buy bouquets which were made at incredible speed by the old market women. Visitors were equally attracted by the fact that several market taverns had a special licence to be open from five in the morning until nine.

'Evening, Arnold,' a porter called from his loading bay. 'Got your rattle handy? I hear you might need it tonight.'

Arnold chuckled. 'Will you come running to my assistance, Charlie?'

'Not me, Arnold. I've got a bad back, haven't I?' He hoisted four crates of Victoria plums onto his shoulder and brought them out to a waiting barrow. 'Besides, Jake Sweeting is bigger than me.'

Arnold helped himself to half a dozen juicy plums and walked on. They looked very mauve in the light from the gas jets, and they felt firm. They tasted delicious.

Jake Sweeting had been a power in the Holy Land until six months ago. Then he had broken into a paper mill in Hampshire and wounded the night watchman with a knife. Jake was not really a subtle villain, but he was strong and ruthless. He had been easily recognisable from the night watchman's description. A few days later, when Jake had arrived back in London, Superintendent Billings had decided that he should be put away.

'Go and arrest him, Pipkin', the Superintendent had ordered.

'Isn't that asking for trouble, sir?'

'He's a cracksman; you'll find enough evidence in his hideout. . . .'

Orange Market, Duke's Place, an obvious temptation to thieves

'I know, sir. But Jake is a powerful man. . . .'

'He's five feet eight inches tall, slightly built, wiry with cropped black hair and a sallow complexion, known to have a vicious temper. He's obviously the man we want!'

Superintendent Billings had wanted to show the Detective Force that his men at Bow Street were first-class thief takers. So Arnold and four other policemen had gone and arrested Jake Sweeting. And it had caused a lot of trouble. When he was gone all the second-rate villains had engaged in bloody, bitter struggles among themselves to decide who was going to run the Holy Land in his place. There had been two pitched battles, a fire, a public house had been wrecked and two girls had been disfigured with acid, and then Noah Clark had established himself as the new leader. It had all been very troublesome. Arnold preferred to let the Holy Land look after itself.

And now the escaped burglar would be wanting to settle his score with Arnold.

'Hey, put that back, you young varmint!'

A ragged street urchin had snatched a pear from the basket right under Arnold's nose. The kid ducked round Arnold's legs and ran off through Bradley's passage. Arnold chased him for twenty yards, just as a gesture, but he had no chance of catching the brat. He returned, puffing awkwardly, to the main street.

'I spy blue, I spy black,' the kid sang out in mockery, 'I spy a peeler in a shiny hat!'

Ratting for the million, from a contemporary painting

Jake Sweeting had got off lightly because, oddly, Arnold had found nothing in the man's hideout to associate him with the burglary at the paper mill. Of course, the night watchman had come on the scene almost at once, and according to him nothing had been taken except a few rolls of blank paper. So Jake had been sentenced to five years' hard labour for nothing.

Jake Sweeting had been a sweep's climbing boy years ago; but sweeps were savage masters, and Jake had early determined to gain his independence. He had graduated to burglary at the age of eleven. He had climbed up chimneys in the daytime for his master, making a mental note of a house's layout and what was worth stealing, and then at night he had returned to climb down the chimney. It had soon become obvious that there was a connection between the robberies and the fact that the victims had all had their chimneys recently cleaned, so Jake's master had been arrested, tried and transported for life. Jake had managed to fend for himself ever since. He had served two short spells in the House of Correction in his youth, but he had kept remarkably free of the law since then. He now owned three lodging houses in St Giles and a house in Hampstead. He could have retired at the age of thirty-five if he had wanted.

Arnold noticed that he had left the smell of fruit behind him and he was back among the smells of the cess pool, boiled clothes and rotten fish. He had reached the edge of the Holy Land again without noticing. Time passes quickly some nights between one and three.

It was still very quiet.

Arnold seldom ventured into the Holy Land beyond Martha Goddard's place. He wasn't a reckless man. He wouldn't even go much further with his cutlass, which was kept at the police station for slicing bread and carrying on parades. Arnold had his own, less direct methods of finding out what was happening in those teeming alleys and tumbledown buildings. He paused on the corner and looked at the notices pasted on the wall of Vine's warehouse. A dog fight was announced for Sunday evening at the Coach and Horses. At the Black Swan the landlord was offering to sell rats to gentlemen.

'Ratting for the Million' the announcement declared. The rats were to be killed in a large wire pit, and a gold watch would be awarded to the owner of the dog that killed the most rats. The entry fee was a shilling. Arnold sighed. Dog fights and ratting attracted a very unruly mob, which did not make a policeman's life any easier. All that betting and brawling and drinking. . . .

A door at the end of the street had opened and somebody had slipped furtively into the white pool of light beneath the gas jets. Arnold watched the man scuttle towards him. He was thick set, hunched in a frock coat and wearing a pork pie hat. It was Noah Clark! Arnold remained in the shadows of Vine's warehouse and watched him pass. Noah's footsteps were muffled almost into silence, but he breathed like one of those new steam engines. He crossed over the road towards New Oxford Street.

'Odd,' Arnold muttered to himself. He was up to no good, obviously, because Noah Clark was always up to no good. But he was also avoiding somebody—somebody in the depths of the Holy Land.

Arnold shrugged his shoulders and resumed his beat. As he turned the corner into Little Earlham Street he heard the approach of a horse's hooves. It must be ten minutes to three. He braced his shoulders and quickened his pace. He tried a couple of shop door handles and flashed his bullseye lantern into Trubshaw's alley.

The man on horseback came abreast of Arnold. 'Whoa!' He reined in his horse.

Arnold saluted smartly. 'Good evening, Inspector. A quiet night. . . .'

'Good evening, Ninety-four. All quiet on beat number four?'

'Yes, sir.'

'Very good. Carry on, Ninety-four.'

The Inspector raised his Field Marshal's baton in acknowledgement and

Covent Garden Market

rode off towards beat number five. It was his nightly tour of the battleground. Arnold carried on, crunch, crunch, crunch, along West Street. The unvarying rhythm of his walk brought Arnold to the door of Martha Goddard's lodging house at three o'clock precisely. It invariably did. He went down the steps and into the kitchen without knocking.

The heat and the smoke in the room were stifling, but Arnold was accus-

tomed to this. His eyes quickly adjusted to the jumping gaslight and he saw Martha herself sitting in her usual high-backed chair by the open range fire. She was a flabby, jovial woman of about fifty with eyes that sparkled. She was wearing a long maroon dress and her top half was enveloped in shawls.

'My goodness, is it three o'clock already?' she asked in a surprisingly high-pitched voice. 'Doesn't the time pass when you're busy?'

She appeared to be busy drinking gin and water. There was nothing else to occupy her, unless she was supervising the three young girls who were sitting across the room at a long wooden table. They were talking and laughing as they made elaborate ladies' hats. Amy Hill was among them, and she gave Arnold a coy little wave.

'Draw up the rocking chair and warm yourself.' Mrs Goddard leaned over the fire and poured Arnold a large cup of hot gin and water. 'Amy, fetch Mr Pipkin a bite to eat. I'm sure he would like some of my baked rabbit pie.'

'You're a thoughtful woman, Martha.' He placed his top hat carefully above the black, smoke-stained range. The pie looked delicious, if a little dry. Arnold pulled off his heavy boots to air his feet. The damp stone floor felt chill through his woollen socks.

'Nobody given you any trouble tonight, Mrs Goddard?' he asked as he did every night, for the sake of form.

'Not a breath, Mr Pipkin,' she answered as always. 'We don't have any trouble now that you keep an eye on us.'

He sipped his drink and sighed as he felt the fire pass down his throat and into his stomach. That was nice! He drained the cup and waited for his head to lighten.

'Things are quiet in the Holy Land tonight,' he said thoughtfully.

'Like the grave,' Mrs Goddard agreed.

'Everybody waiting to see what Jake Sweeting will do when he arrives.'

'I suppose so; when he arrives.'

They could hear footsteps approaching in the yard outside. The footsteps stopped, and a whispered consultation seemed to be taking place. Then the the door was unlatched and Vicky Corbett came in with a seedy, threadbare young man who took one look at Arnold and tried to bolt. 'Don't be a silly boy,' said Vicky. 'This is only Mr Pipkin.' She pulled the youth into the kitchen and closed the door. 'Go on through, you know the way.' The door leading upstairs to the rest of the house with its maze of rooms and passages opened into total darkness. The young man vanished, but Vicky paused at the door and then returned to whisper in Martha Goddard's ear.

'What, here?' said Martha in dismay. 'Who saw him?'

The girl's answer was lost to Arnold. She went upstairs. Arnold waited for the news.

'Jake Sweeting,' said Mrs Goddard, 'is back in the Holy Land.'

Arnold dozed fitfully by Martha Goddard's fire for half an hour. He didn't actually sleep, because after all he was on duty. But he let his mind flit dreamily over the night's events, and he relaxed.

Mrs Goddard thought that he was in danger. But a policeman's life was safer now than it had been in the old days. In 1829 when the force had first been formed there had been hostility from the entire country. Some of the gentry had refused to pay the New Police Rate of 8d in the £1, and crowds had gathered in the streets to pelt 'Peel's bloody gang' with rotten fruit. The aristocrats had been the worst in those days. They had encouraged their coachmen to lash out at policemen with their whips, and several policemen had been deliberately run over. Earl Waldegrave had persuaded a young prizefighter to entertain the crowd in Piccadilly by beating up and almost killing P.C. William McKenzie. On another occasion Waldegrave and his friend Captain Duff had amused themselves by holding 224 P.C. Charles Wheatley on the ground while their coach was driven over him. Wheatley had been so badly maimed that he had never worked again.

Things had improved gradually. When Arnold had joined the force in 1840 his friends had thought it odd but not actually disreputable. They had understood the attraction of a steady, reliable job that brought in a regular twenty-one shillings a week. Arnold's wife had thought it was a career! She had wanted Arnold to have a respectable position in the community and had fully expected him to rise to the position of superintendent.

She had misunderstood Arnold's character.

'Mr Pipkin,' Martha Goddard said, patting him on the shoulder, 'time to wake up. It's four o'clock.'

'I wasn't asleep. . . .'

'You were snoring.' The girls all squealed with laughter at Arnold's attempts to look wide awake. 'Time to be back on your beat, Mr Pipkin.'

Arnold shuddered as he returned to the cold night air. He called good night to Mrs Goddard and the girls. Only two hours to go and the night would be over. He went briskly up the steps and into Lumber Court. The market came alive again at four, with all the buyers streaming in, shopkeepers and hoteliers and more street traders. There were more traffic jams as well.

'Good evening, Nellie,' he called to a friendly costerwoman.

'God bless you, Mr Pipkin.'

A half-eaten peach hurtled past Arnold's top hat and splattered against the wall. Martha Goddard had been right about the danger Arnold was risking! He spun round and shook his fist at a young street urchin. The small boy dodged between the wheels of a huge cart being drawn by four horses. Arnold muttered, and continued his progress. He was feeling tense again as he reached the Seven Dials. He tried not to think about Jake Sweeting. He decided to think about the Seven Dials. There had been a Doric pillar in the middle of the road, where the seven streets met, and it had been taken down because of a legend that treasure was buried at the base. But nobody had found any treasure, so the pillar had been taken away to be re-erected in Weybridge.

Arnold glanced carefully up and down Monmouth Street. It was a clothes

23

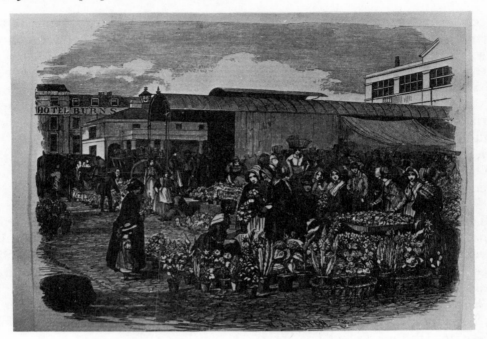

The flower market, Covent Garden

market during the day. But there was no sign of life now. He continued along West Street.

It was twenty minutes past four when he noticed the crimson glow rising from the sky behind Bill Kellow's bakery. 'Oh no,' he said apprehensively, 'not a fire!' But the glow seemed to be mixed with a flickering yellow. And as he hurried back along his beat he heard the strident clatter of Sam Quine's hand rattle. 'Confound the wretched man,' Arnold muttered. Somebody had raised the alarm, some busybody lurking about doing mischief. A policeman who discovered a fire 'without first having his attention called to it by anyone' was paid ten shillings. However, Arnold could still earn an extra shilling by making certain that all windows and doors of the burning building remained shut until the fire brigade arrived.

The fire was in Monmouth Court, and already the blaze had spread through the building. It was an old clothes factory next door to Jem Catnach's printing works, and from the look of it the clothes were burning furiously. Arnold judged it would take another hour to be completely gutted, and then the buildings on either side would be ablaze as well.

Half a dozen bedraggled figures were huddled on the street corner watching the flames. 'Have you seen anybody at the windows?' Arnold demanded. 'Have the doors been opened?'

'It's all right, Arnold, nobody has stirred.'

'Thank God.' Arnold mopped his face with his spotted silk handkerchief. It was often difficult to persuade people to stay in a burning building—they would try to escape or save their belongings; but it was vital to keep all the doors and windows shut to prevent fires from spreading. 'Kit Oldcastle, I want you to go. . . .'

'It's all been done, Arnold.' Kit Oldcastle was an ancient beggar who had once been a prosperous lodging-house keeper; he was always around, and he always knew everything. He had sent a man to fetch the fire brigade, another man to summon the fire escape, and a third to awaken the turncock, who would turn on the water supply.

'Oh.' Arnold watched the blaze for a few moments. It was his duty to stay with the fire now, unless it was necessary to give assistance elsewhere. It was his job to control the crowds. But since there were no crowds yet he decided to help Sam Quine. He set off at a trot down St Martin's Lane.

Arnold seldom ran anywhere, but this was an emergency. The Fire Escape Society paid five shillings to the person who gave the call. Arnold had lost that five shillings, but he might still collect half a crown if he and Sam Quine could reach the fire with the escape apparatus before the fire engine. There was a small knot of people on the corner of Trafalgar Square when Arnold arrived. 'Stand back,' he called.

Sam Quine sat in his sentry box on the corner of Trafalgar Square every night between 8 p.m. and 7 a.m., with his fire escape beside him. This was a thirty-five-foot ladder mounted on massive wheels. There was a twenty-foot extension hinged from the top of this main ladder, and there was also a sixteen-foot extension which was carried beneath the carriage. It was a difficult piece of equipment to take through the streets, specially when the canvas chute for people to jump into billowed out and caught the wind like a sail.

'You've taken long enough to get here,' Sam Quine complained. He had been a colour sergeant in the army, and since the Fire Escape Society had been formed in 1828 Quine had been standing in this sentry box every night like a man deserted by his regiment.

'Let's get moving,' said Arnold. 'We don't want the fire engine to be there first!' He pointed to the two largest men among the bystanders. 'You and you, help us with this equipment. Take it from the rear. . . .'

'Excuse me, Constable Pipkin,' said Quine, 'but this is my Fire Escape Station. I give the orders.' He removed the cap which bore the initials F.E.S. and put on his helmet, then he turned to the same two men. 'You and you. Can I have your assistance, please?' Quine's instructions were that a policeman should be his principal helper if a policeman were available, but Quine was still in charge.

Sergeant Quine led his team at a steady canter back along St Martin's Lane, pushing the ladder before them and drawing the crowd behind. It was a heavy burden, and soon they were jogging more slowly. By the time they reached Monmouth Court the fire engine had arrived and the leather hose was already connected to the fire hydrant fifty yards away. The reward would be only one shilling and sixpence now, with a shilling each for the other two volunteers.

'Couldn't you have imagined you were running away from the enemy?' Arnold asked Sam Quine. 'You might have moved more quickly.'

'It was your fault,' said Quine. 'You should have been pushing with the rest of us instead of just hanging on for the ride.'

The horse which had drawn the fire engine had been unhitched and was idly chewing the posters on the wall of Vine's warehouse. Arnold pushed his way through the crowd. 'Anybody inside there?' he asked the foreman of the fire engine.

'Not a chance,' the man answered. 'If there was anybody in that furnace he'd be a dead 'un by now.'

There was a crash of splitting timber and then slowly in the leaping yellow light a brick wall leaned over into the fire. It seemed to take nearly a minute to fall, leaving an iron window frame suspended on a red-hot girder. The audience gasped.

'Better rescue the people next door,' Arnold shouted to Quine. 'The fire might spread!'

'I don't need you to tell me my job!'

Luckily there was too much noise from the flames for an argument to develop. Arnold helped to wheel the fire escape to the next building. The occupants of the premises—a butcher's shop—were already in the street, but it was, as Sam Quine observed, best to make certain. Arnold strolled back to the fire engine with a few calls of 'Keep clear there,' to the gathering crowd. The foreman of the engine had already gathered his first sixteen volunteers to help with the pump, and they were lined up eight on each side of the engine, hands to the bar and ready to haul.

'Right,' said the foreman pointing to the first side, 'down with the pump!' They hauled down and the foreman pointed to the other side. 'Down with the pump!' They hauled. 'Down with the pump!'

The glistening red fire engine was a hand-operated machine which worked on two cylinders. It had been built by Mr Merryweather of Long Acre, who had just begun making the new steam engine that worked without all these volunteer pumpers. But it would never catch on; it took so long to get up steam, and it meant no shilling reward or free beer for the helpers, so

Fire escapes with a
horse-drawn fire engine

naturally the bystanders were tempted to cut the hoses and cause obstructions when they found a steam engine being used. Steam engines had been tried before.

'Beer oh,' called the volunteers as they hauled down on one side, and 'beer oh,' responded the others as they hauled back.

'Beer oh, beer oh,' the chant continued. The firemen themselves directed the jet of water onto the blazing ruins of the clothing factory and supervised the rescue of property from the other buildings which were threatened. Then they smashed down the doors and wooden fences that were likely to catch fire as the flames spread. There was no hope for the clothing factory; they were trying now to limit the destruction. Arnold only hoped that there were no explosive chemicals in Jem Catnach's printing works.

Supervising fires was exhausting work, and Arnold was grateful to see the beer arriving for the volunteer pumpers. The first sixteen men were relieved by a second shift and went across to collect their pints. Arnold joined them.

'Beer oh,' the second shift began chanting, 'beer oh!'

'Down with the pump!'

Arnold took a deep swig of his beer. It was thirsty work. He offered up a silent thanksgiving that London was unlike some provincial towns where the fire brigade was the local police force. The London Fire Engine Establishment had been formed in 1832 by an amalgamation of the old insurance brigades, and it provided a system which worked very well for Arnold. He would earn an extra three shillings and sixpence for tonight's work, plus all the beer he wanted.

Arnold noticed that dawn was coming up across the city already. He would soon be off duty. It would soon be time for him to make his calls.

2. *MORNING*

'Mr Seaford!' Arnold hammered on the man's door. 'Mr Seaford. Half past six, sir. Good morning to you.'

Mr Seaford poked a sleepy head out of the first-floor window. 'All right, Constable. I'm obliged to you.'

Arnold waved cheerily and went off to waken Mr O'Gorman. There were eight calls on his walk back to Bow Street, and they each paid Arnold four-pence a week to be roused in the mornings. Mr McEnroe was the trouble-some one—he usually had a hangover. Once Mr McEnroe had gone back to sleep and then refused to pay the fourpence at the end of the week; Arnold made a point now of going into the man's lodgings and if necessary tipping him out of his bed.

As he neared Bow Street he met up with several other policemen coming off duty. They grunted amiably at each other. Arnold found his fellow policemen a stolid, unimaginative bunch. More than half of them were ex-army, and they seemed to have joined the force because it was better than working. Most of them lived in station lodgings and had never felt the need to look after themselves. But there were others, ex-farm labourers and butchers and blacksmiths, men like Arnold himself from the country, married men with normal responsibilities.

'I hear you've had a fire in Monmouth Court,' said 202 P.C. John Jones. He fell into step beside Arnold.

'It's all under control now,' Arnold said modestly. 'Nobody was hurt.'

'I had a fire up in Pheonix Street a fortnight ago. . . .'

A London coffee stall

29

The old police court in Bow Street in 1881

'Yes,' said Arnold. 'I remember.' Phoenix Street was just to the north of Arnold's beat.

'I don't like fires. A fourteen-year-old girl was burnt to death. . . .'

'I know, you told me.' Arnold did not like thinking about such things.

'And old Mrs Harding was killed. There were six families living in that house, all rushing about with their nightclothes alight and screaming with pain. Three of them are still in hospital.'

'Yes,' Arnold said uneasily. 'You told me. This was only old Moses Arenson's sweat shop. Nobody was hurt.'

'Moses Arenson?' John Jones chewed thoughtfully at his moustache. 'Was the place insured against fire? Because if it was you can be certain that Moses set fire to it himself. He's a villain, Moses Arenson. He makes more money than a sweat-shop owner can make honestly from selling clothes.'

'Perhaps,' Arnold said reluctantly. 'But I like him. He's an amusing villain.'

They went into Bow Street police station together. It was a relatively new building on the same side of the road as the Royal Italian Opera House. It had been rebuilt in 1825, opposite the old offices from which Henry Fielding had first administered his Bow Street Runners. Those offices had been almost destroyed during the Gordon Riots.

They passed the wooden barrier and went along the dim passage into the general office. The assorted policemen gathered to make their reports to their sergeants, and while they did so the route papers were continuously being brought in from other metropolitan stations. Route papers were reports of crimes, incidents, missing persons, deaths, which were copied out and then passed on to the next police station. The first thing that had struck Arnold when he had joined the force was that it involved a lot of paperwork. The far side of the office was taken up with a large barracks-style bedstead; Sergeant Green was asleep on it, after his night spent returning from Cambridge with an escaped prisoner. On the left a section of the room was railed off for prisoners, and a window on the right opened onto Inspector Drew's administrative office.

The buzz of gossip continued. Half a dozen starving children had been brought in during the night and were on their way to the union workhouse; some twenty-three cases of drunk and disorderly were in the cells; two men had been beaten and robbed, an old man had been knocked down by a horse, a burglary had taken place in Hart Street. . . .

'Ah, Pipkin,' said his sergeant. 'Wait behind afterwards, will you? The Inspector wants a word with you.'

Arnold sighed and sat on the bed beside Sergeant Green's feet. He listened to the scratching of the quill pen as Sergeant Collins filled out the Metropolitan Police Register for the Bow Street, E Division. From this was

Conducting the night's charges to the police court

compiled the massive 'Morning State of the Metropolitan Police Force' which recorded the number of superintendents, inspectors, sergeants and constables on duty in the whole of London, which showed whether the absentees were sick or on leave, and gave information about the horses. Arnold's gaze strayed across to the 'Found Dead' blackboard.

'I see you're still alive then, Pipkin,' said 269 P.C. Fred Cathcart. He sat heavily on the bed beside Arnold.

'Yes.'

'I thought an escaped prisoner was after you.' Fred Cathcart lit a clay pipe and filled the air with tobacco smoke before commenting further. 'The trouble with prisons these days,' he said eventually, 'is that they're too soft. Like being in a model lodging house. Everything free, warders to look after you and a nice warm bed. I suppose Jake Sweeting became bored with all the luxury.'

'Very likely.'

'It's not surprising that nobody respects the law,' Cathcart continued. 'These reformers have taken all the fun out of justice. How often do you see a public hanging these days? Or a beheading?'

'Very rarely,' Arnold agreed.

'They've abolished the stocks and public whippings. No wonder people have lost interest in the law.'

'Quite,' said Arnold. 'They're too soft on prisoners these days.'

'No wonder Jake Sweeting hopped it.'

The office had gradually emptied, and there were now only the six reserve constables waiting around to answer the calls which came in during the day. The place was quiet except for the snores of Sergeant Green. Inspector Drew put his head through the connecting window and gestured to Arnold.

'Pipkin. Will you come through?'

'Yes, sir.'

Arnold shuffled to attention behind the large oak desk and saluted.

'Ninety-four, I've been looking over your record, and you've arrested only ten people this last month. Is that doing your duty?'

'Yes, sir, I think so.' Arnold held his breath while the Inspector marched forward, stared into his face and then marched back round his desk. 'I know that we pick up five or six thousand children a year, and I know that we charge more than seven thousand people for criminal offences—of which half are for being drunk and disorderly. But my beat is up in the Holy Land. . . .'

Inspector Drew sniffed so alarmingly that Arnold's voice tailed off into silence. There was a dreadful pause. 'Have you been drinking, Ninety-four?'

'Certainly not, sir. A small refreshment while I was assisting at the fire, that was all. But it sustained me, sir, don't worry, I shall be able to carry out my duties.'

'You're lazy, Pipkin!'

'Yes, sir. But if I started arresting every homeless child and calling him a vagrant you would need to build a dozen new prisons just for the kids in the Holy Land.' He thought of Fearless Sergeant Jenkins, who was always arresting five-year-old children for serious breaches of the peace such as begging; several times Jenkins had reached Bow Street with a screaming infant by the scruff of the neck surrounded by a jeering crowd of market porters. 'Was that all, sir?'

Inspector Drew stared into his face again. 'No, it isn't. I don't like drunkenness.'

'Neither do I, sir. But if I started arresting every drunk I meet. . . .'

'Shut up!'

'Yes, sir.'

'I've received a complaint from Lord Warren that it took him half an hour to drive from the opera to New Oxford Street last night. He said the traffic in Covent Garden was so congested that he was late for his supper engagement!'

Arnold laughed, but he quickly smothered it pretending that it was a tickle

33

in his throat. He coughed, and muttered something about doing his best to keep the streets clear.

'I'm pleased to hear it. All right, you can go, now.' Drew waited until Arnold had reached the door before saying, 'By the way, I see that this fellow Sweeting escaped from the Steel yesterday. Do you know where he might be?'

'Yes, sir,' Arnold said proudly. 'He's in the Holy Land, resting up at his place in Cat Alley.'

'I see.' The Inspector glanced across the room at a sergeant who was writing at a desk. But the sergeant was absorbed in his work. 'Have you tried to arrest him yet?'

Arnold gaped in astonishment. 'No, sir. Cat Alley is not on my beat, and I don't go into the Holy Land by myself. We would need a dozen men. . . .'

'All right, thank you, Ninety-four. Carry on, and let me see a few more arrests on your record.'

Arnold found that it was half past eight already. It was time for breakfast. He went off to Mac's place in Long Acre. Arnold's breakfasts in the kitchen of Alexander Mackintosh's Long Acre hotel were part of the arrangement he had with the chef to keep the hotel out of trouble. Arnold was not at all sure what kind of trouble they expected, but so long as they were prepared to give him and P.C. Wilkins a free breakfast below stairs he was not too particular.

£50 REWARD
ABSCONDED
On the Afternoon of Saturday, the 30th inst. between the hours of 3 & 4, a Young Man, from the Office of Mr. Ford, Henrietta St. Covent Garden, with

900 SOVEREIGNS.

His name is Edmund Pott, he is about 25 years of age, 5 feet 10 high, pale Complexion, light Hair and Eyes, rather thick set, slow in his speech, has rather a downcast look, was dressed all in black, with Wellington Boots when he left, writes a neat but mercantile hand. He is an Englishman, but speaks the Italian, German and French Languages.

Whoever will give such Information as will lead to his apprehension to Mr. G. S. Ford, No. 8, Henrietta Street, Covent Garden, London, shall receive the above Reward.

SATURDAY, SEPT. 30, 1837.

Alfred Robins, Typ., Tavistock Street, Covent Garden.

A reward notice of the kind which is still posted outside police stations today

An hour later Arnold Pipkin was fit to resume work. He went back up the steps and into the police station. He could tell at once that something important was happening. Inspector Drew's door was closed, and two constables in the general office were sitting tensely silent. They gestured anxiously at Arnold, as though otherwise he might burst into song.

'Top-level conference,' whispered 269 P.C. Cathcart. 'The superintendent himself and a nob from Scotland Yard are in there.' He waited until Arnold was settled on the bed beside the still snoring Sergeant Green. 'Kit Oldcastle was in here half an hour ago. He was very agitated.'

Everybody was agitated this morning. Arnold nodded. 'What was the matter with him?'

'They've found some charred remains in Moses Arenson's factory. It seems that somebody was burned to death after all.'

'Has Moses turned up?'

'Kit didn't mention him.' Fred Cathcart laughed uneasily. 'When Moses does arrive on the scene he'll set up the loudest wailing wall since the sacking of Jerusalem!'

Which was true. Arnold wondered whether he should have gone straight round to Moses' place in Drury Lane, but he disliked so much excitement. 'I'll break the news to him when I'm finished here.'

Inspector Drew appeared in the doorway. 'Pipkin, will you come through?'

Arnold wondered why such important people should wish to see him. The man from Scotland Yard was Detective Inspector Charles Field; he was standing in the shadows of Drew's office and his eyes seemed to catch the yellow glint from the gasfire. Superintendent Billings was sitting in the frame of the window sill like a Biblical prophet, with the light behind him. There was another man present as well; a thin, energetic man with a face like parchment and a gravel voice; nobody introduced him.

'Ninety-four,' said Inspector Drew, 'how well do you know Dudley Street?'

'Very well indeed,' Arnold said rashly.

'Splendid. The Superintendent wants you to take a party of detectives in there this evening. Inspector Field will be conducting the raid, and I've offered him your full support.'

Arnold grunted. If the raid went according to plan it would all be due to Inspector Field's brilliance, and if things went wrong it would be Arnold's fault. Either way it would be physically dangerous. 'Dudley Street in Islington?' he enquired.

'Dudley Street in Seven Dials, you idiot!'

'Oh.' Arnold beamed helpfully. 'You mean the Dudley Street on P.C. Jones' beat?'

'That's right. But your sergeant says you know the people in the Holy Land much better than Jones does. He says, and we all know it for a fact, that you have the confidence of those people.'

The reason Jones didn't have their confidence was that he kept trying to arrest them. Arnold asked what the raid was designed to achieve.

'The Detective Force are hunting for a criminal whom we know to be hiding out behind Dudley Street, and the officer of the Royal Mint, Mr Brennan, is convinced that the raid will mop up a gang of forgers. But they need the co-operation,' said Superintendent Billings, 'of the man on the beat.'

'I see,' Arnold said.

'Inspector Drew has discovered that Jake Sweeting has gone to ground in Cat Alley,' the superintendent continued. 'So we must move in now, before the gang can reorganise its operation elsewhere.'

Arnold smiled. He knew of no connection between Jake Sweeting and any forgery ring. Jake was a big-time burglar! 'With due respect to Mr Brennan,' he pointed out, 'there isn't enough money in coining to attract Jake Sweeting. A silver five shilling piece sells for fourpence at the current rate and half crowns go for threepence halfpenny. There's no profit in it for anybody. The prisons are full of people who've been caught in the pubs and on racecourses passing dud coins. Why would Jake bother?'

'We think,' said Mr Brennan, 'that his organisation has been making its own bank notes—or as they would call it, doing a bit of soft.'

Inspector Field emerged from the shadows and pointed a significant finger along the side of his nose. 'Mr Sweeting is a clever criminal, Constable. He has solved the greatest problem which faces a forger of bank notes. Do you know what that is?'

Arnold knew several problems. The printing press weighed more than a ton and was difficult to conceal. The engraver had to be a superb craftsman. But Inspector Field had not waited for an answer to his question.

'The problem has always been in the paper. The forgers have used paper that was *similar* to Bank of England material, but it has not been the same. The watermark has been missing. Of course, good forgers have sometimes added a watermark to the surface of the paper, but than can always be washed off.' Inspector Field looked dramatically round at his audience. 'So how has Jake Sweeting solved that problem?'

Arnold waited to be told the answer.

'Jake Sweeting stole a quantity of the genuine paper from the Bank of England's own suppliers.' He tapped his left temple meaningfully. 'You see, genuine paper with the proper watermark. And that makes any forgery undetectable.'

Arnold gaped at his superintendent while the pieces of puzzle fell one by one into place. So *that* was why Jake Sweeting had stolen the rolls of blank paper from Portal's. The man was a genius!

'Has any of this undetectable forged money passed into circulation?' he asked.

'How would we know, you idiot?'

Yes, Arnold reflected, he hadn't thought of that.

'All right, Pipkin,' said the Superintendent. 'You can go home and get some rest. We'll see you at nine o'clock this evening.'

'Yes, sir.' Arnold raised his hand in salute and then left.

There was a small crowd of people assembled on the pavement outside. They were obviously waiting for something. Eyes turned towards the alley beside the police court. Arnold stopped to watch with the rest of them. At that moment 'Her Majesty's carriage' came clattering along the street. It was a covered vehicle to take prisoners sentenced that morning to gaol. The coachman drew up at the office door. The crowd pushed closer, leaving a narrow corridor for the prisoners. Two young women came out first, followed by a small boy who was crying and a red-faced man who looked as though he had been very drunk the night before.

'Come on! In with you!' called the coachman.

People in the crowd called out to the two girls. 'What did you get, Nellie?' and 'Off to the Steel again?' The girls were defiant, proud, and climbed

This type of 'black maria' came into use in 1858, although this photograph outside prison was taken sometime around 1900

37

laughing into the coach. The small boy was less in control of himself, and as the coachman lifted him aboard he bit the man's hand.

'You street urchin,' snarled the coachman. 'They'll teach you how to behave where you're going!'

Arnold patted the horses thoughtfully on the nose and continued on his way.

3. AT HOME

Arnold Pipkin had his lodgings in Red Lion Street, nearly a mile from the police station. He set off homewards shortly before midday, turning east down Long Acre and across Drury Lane. He stopped on his way to call at Moses Arenson's rooms in Chesney Buildings, but Moses was not at home. Several faces appeared at the windows opposite, and a small boy sitting among the litter at the foot of the steps watched suspiciously. Arnold knocked again while a half-starved mongrel growled at his ankles. It was a rough neighbourhood, filled with the smells of food and decaying rubbish, but it was law-abiding compared with the Holy Land.

'Moses done a bunk,' the small boy volunteered at last.

'Ah, gone away, eh?' Arnold bent down and patted the mongrel on the head. 'Do you know where I can find him? I'm afraid there's been trouble at his factory. . . .'

'Yea, they burnt it down, didn't they?' He laughed unsympathetically, and called the dog Trixie across to him. 'I don't know where he's gone. He just done a bunk yesterday afternoon.'

'Is that so?' Arnold sat on the steps beside the boy. 'Did he seem upset or excited when he went?'

'Moses Arenson excited? He's always excited!'

Arnold took a penny from his pocket and looked at it doubtfully. 'So we don't know where Mr Arenson went to, eh? That's a pity. I wanted particularly to find him.'

The boy looked eagerly at the coin. 'They did say as how he'd gone to Birmingham,' he said, taking the penny. 'But now it don't seem likely. They say they found a corpse all burnt to a cinder in the fire.'

As Arnold plodded steadily home he felt the burden of his work lifting from his shoulders, as if he were leaving crime and traffic jams and police inspectors behind. Red Lion Street was a teeming, tumbledown thoroughfare full of noise and smells and people much the same as the streets behind Drury Lane, but it had the advantage of being a mile away. This was a separate life.

'Good morning, Mrs Moynihan,' he called. 'Glorious morning!'

'Hello, Arnold,' she shouted down from the window. 'End of a busy night?' She was a large-boned, friendly woman who beat up her husband every

Saturday night when he was drunk. She had seven children and an eighth on the way, but she remained cheerful.

'Yes, pretty active. How about you?'

'Yes, pretty active.' Her laughter rang out across the street. Her husband had been a navigator, as the manual labourers were called, on the railways, until the mania for building railways had died down a couple of years ago. Arnold had not liked to enquire what he did now.

'Off to bed, Arnold?' called the local butcher. 'What about taking the wife home some tripe as a nice surprise?'

Even the dogs were friendly in Red Lion Street; a shaggy-coated black spaniel wagged its tail as Arnold turned into the inappropriately named Bishop's Mansions. There was always a lot of activity outside, people laughing or fighting and children chasing each other and street traders bawling their wares, as if nobody ever closed their doors on the world. The only person who did not altogether join in with the noisy warmth of the neighbourhood was Arnold's wife. She thought the brash life of the streets was vulgar. She was probably right. She preferred the restraint, the respectability she had been used to in Godalming.

Edith Pipkin was a slight, restrained woman whose mother had been the village schoolmistress; Edith's sister was at a ragged school and her three brothers were all doing well 'in business'. They had been an ambitious family, and it was Edith's misfortune that she had directed most of her ambitions into Arnold. She had brought him as far as London, but she had not been able to make him a success.

'I'm home, Edith,' he called.

'You're late,' she said severely. She was a neat, trim, tightly corseted woman with her black hair pulled back in a bun. She was the same age as Arnold, but obviously destined to live on after him to be ninety.

Arnold was late four days out of five, because of court appearances and briefing sessions and emergencies on his beat, but Edith always expected him home at nine o'clock. 'The Superintendent wanted to see me.'

'Did you tell him you should be promoted?'

'No. It didn't seem the right occasion.' Arnold put eighteen shillings on the table beside her. He was paid on Wednesdays when he went on duty, and he always made a point of handing over the money intact to Edith. Twenty-one shilling gross, less two shillings for his uniform and a shilling stoppages this week. He let Edith handle the money side of their marriage.

'I'll make some tea,' she said, 'while you're getting ready for bed.'

Arnold's father had been a farm labourer; he had gone to work when day broke and had come home when it was dark. From the age of eight Arnold had gone with him and had earned four shillings a week scaring birds away from the newly sown corn. Arnold hadn't learned to read until many years later. But it had been a happy childhood—it had been what Arnold (in those reflective periods on his beat) called 'natural'. He would have been quite content to remain in Godalming all his life, ploughing fields and sowing corn, bringing in the harvest, drinking at the village inn, taking the rhythm of his days from nature. But he had met Edith. As a result they were living in two rooms in Red Lion Street, and Edith complained continually of the over-crowding. The furniture had all been shabby when they acquired it; they made do, mended, mended, and made do. The rooms were shabby, but impeccably clean. It was not entirely to Arnold's taste, but he had a lot to be grateful for.

Arnold would have liked a framed pokerwork inscription above their bed, like most people had. 'The primary object of an efficient Police,' it would read, 'is the Prevention of crime—The next that of Detection and punishment of offenders if a crime is committed. To these ends all efforts of Police should be directed. The protection of life and property and the preservation of public tranquillity.' But Edith didn't like pokerwork, and she refused to embroider it on a sampler either.

'I don't care if it *was* said by Sir Richard Mayne, I'm not having tasteless decorations in our home!' Ever since she had discovered that Mrs Moynihan had 'Home Sweet Home' above the fireplace and a tinted engraving of Queen Victoria and Prince Albert over her bed Edith had developed a dislike of such frivolity in the home. 'If Mrs Moynihan went to sleep instead of closing her eyes and thinking of England she'd be a lot better off!' Edith had declared. Somehow all of Mrs Pipkin's views and principles added to the sombreness of their life. The furniture was all brown, the kitchen and its utensils, the iron, the kettle and the fireplace were black and were continually being given an extra blackening.

Arnold stood in his flannel nightshirt by the bed. He could hear the noises of the street outside, and brilliant sunshine was trying to penetrate the small, clean lattice windows. He was deep in thought and hardly noticed that Edith had come in with his tea.

'What did the Superintendent want to see you about?' she asked.

'The Detective Force are making a raid on the Holy Land tonight. They want me to go in with them.' He smiled. 'I suppose it shows they trust me. They aren't sending Jack Jones because he'd wreck the whole operation.'

'If they trust you they could make you a sergeant.'

'I'm not the type.' Arnold put his arm round her shoulders. 'Can you imagine me shouting out orders, left right left right, putting all my friends on charges?' He chuckled.

'You'd be paid more money.'

'We're very lucky to get a guinea a week,' Arnold said gently. 'I saw in your paper the other day that cotton workers in Oldham are paid four shillings a week. We're lucky.'

'I know,' she said wearily, 'and your father received ten shillings a week till the day he died. But I can't manage on what you give me.'

Edith was mindful of what Sir Robert Peel himself had said a few years ago in Parliament. 'I have good reason for thinking that one of my police constables, if a single man, can find out of his pay of a guinea a week: 1. lodgings, 2. medical attendance, 3. very comfortable subsistence at his mess, 4. clothing; and can, after finding these save out of his pay ten shillings a week.' When Edith had first heard that she had accused Arnold of spending the spare ten shillings on drink! That was why he now handed over his pay intact.

Arnold was a placid sort of character, but the suggestion that he had been spending his wages on drink had filled him with indignation. Arnold sometimes spent money from the tips and rewards and the payments for his morning calls on such things, but Edith knew little of this extra income. Besides in Arnold's opinion they ought to drink beer at home. There had been another cholera epidemic in the city last year, which had probably been caused by pollution of the water supplies. But Edith put morality above health, and they continued to drink water from a fly-blown water butt.

She spent 5s 6d on rent, 5s on bread, 1s on flour, 1s on tea, 8d on sugar, 1s 4d on potatoes, 1s $4\frac{1}{2}$d on butter, 2d on pepper and salt, 9d on cheese, 1s 4d on wood and coal, 4d on candles, $3\frac{1}{2}$d on milk, $4\frac{1}{2}$d on soap; which left very little for meat, clothing, medicine and magazines.

'You ought to look around for a better job,' said Edith.

But it was too late. A man can't change his career and start again when he's forty. And in fact Arnold had no desire for change. He climbed into bed feeling something like contentment. The worries over money were nothing to do with him, and he had no desire to be a divisional superintendent. He kissed Edith on the forehead and murmured good night. Within half a minute he was sleeping like a chubby, strong, red-faced baby.

Edith deserved better than all this, Arnold realised. He had let her down. She was a natural teacher; she had begun teaching him to read when he was eighteen, and within two years he could read and write like a schoolboy. His hand at the police station was clearer than that of any man below the rank of inspector. A constable had to be able to read and write to qualify for the job, so he owed his position to Edith. He read Edith's *Punch* and her *Illustrated London News* every week. He didn't think *Punch* was funny (it was always making jokes about policemen) and he was none too keen on the illustrations in the *Illustrated London News*.

Arnold preferred the *Illustrated Police News*, which some of the men at the station read. It was a sensational magazine, not to be confused with the official *Police Gazette*. The *Illustrated Police News* was full of murders and suicides and sensational violence; it made police work seem much more exciting than Arnold's own humdrum view of the job.

Perhaps Arnold was lacking in a sense of humour. He had never forgiven *Punch* for writing that 'policemen's boots are of two sizes only, the too small and the too large. The latter class are by far the most numerous; so that it is easy to judge a policeman by his foot which seems about twice as big as anyone else's.' Arnold took size nine boots, but he could see that Colonel Rowan was right in selecting new recruits according to their feet first and their character second. There was a lot of walking to be done in a peeler's life. Arnold soaked his feet in vinegar every day, because he believed it strengthened the soles and prevented them from smelling.

Arnold had been wakened by the Yorkshire cake man; it was six o'clock in the evening. He yawned, and swung his feet out of bed. Another busy day about to begin.

> Yorkshire cakes, Who'll buy Yorkshire cakes,
> All piping hot—smoking hot! hot!

The man came round every Thursday evening and his voice echoed through the street like a bugle call. He could be heard 300 yards away even when he was simply giving somebody change for sixpence. Arnold began dressing.

It was a disadvantage of a policeman's life that he had to wear his uniform on duty and off. Edith used to say that if she ever saw her husband in a wing collar and bow tie she wouldn't recognise him—she would run to the window and scream for the police. But Arnold had grown accustomed to it. He pulled on his white summer trousers. There was the traditional grease mark against the hip. You could always recognise an old peeler by the grease mark where the bullseye lantern hung on his belt. Arnold struggled for the usual ten minutes with his collar before going next door and asking Edith to fix it. It was four inches wide, made of leather and covered with black silk. It was designed to prevent anybody from strangling him and took several months to get used to.

'Your supper won't be ready for another ten minutes,' said Edith. 'You'd better sit and read for a while.' She waved towards the copy of *Rural Rides* on the sideboard. 'I've been reading Mr Cobbett again. He's so good on the English countryside. He reminds me of home.' For a moment Edith looked at Arnold as though they were eighteen again. Her brown eyes were deep and full of tenderness, but then she turned away, bustling and clattering as she prepared the evening meal.

Edith was still trying to improve her husband, even though Arnold was forty-two and a disappointment. She had been sending him off to the new Mechanics' Institute to learn about famous men and foreign countries and the British Constitution. Arnold had attended more than a dozen lectures in the past year, some of which had been interesting. But he was still a constable on the beat. Knowledge was not necessarily a gateway to success. In fact Arnold had his doubts about the value of knowledge. He had not told Edith, but at one lecture, on the evils of crime, Arnold had positively disgraced himself. He had argued with the lecturer.

The Reverend Anthony Blanchard had been instructing the audience on the moral benefits of Pentonville Prison and the fact that idleness is at the root of all evil. He had criticised the appearance of criminals, attributing 'surly brutality' to one and 'stupid insensibility' to another. And he had concluded that those who will not work were the pests of our society. He had attacked the vagrants, the tramps, the beggars and rogues who were destined for the new model gaol as though they preferred gaol to honest work.

Arnold had thought this misleading. He had tried to point out that most of the lawlessness in London was caused by people (costers, tinkers, navvies, sweeps, street traders and entertainers) who worked very hard indeed. 'And where can those who have no work go to find respectable employment?' Arnold asked him. 'I know hundreds of people who beg and cheat because they can't find work. They don't choose to be idle. . . .'

'Are you denying that those who presently lie rotting in our gaols would be there if they had been gainfully employed?'

'Well, no,' Arnold had said in confusion.

'So why should you offer your approval at the sight of sweeps and navvies brawling in the streets?'

'I don't,' Arnold began.

'We shall not solve the evil by leaving it to God, my man. We must understand the viciousness in ourselves that leads to the appalling crime in our society.' And so on. Arnold had decided that learning, when it dealt with something you had not had practical experience of, was pretty useless. He preferred facts. There were 5435 people at that moment in prisons in London. That was a fact. Except that Jake Sweeting had escaped yesterday.

'Supper's ready,' called Edith.

'Ah,' said Arnold, 'the smell of it has been making me hungry.'

'For what we are about to receive may the Lord make us truly thankful.'

'Amen.'

'Did you have a busy time last night, Arnold?' She believed the evening meal was an occasion for family talk, so that wholesome food and conversation would strengthen the bonds of marriage. Arnold told her about the fire and tiresome Sam Quine, about Jake Sweeting's escape. 'I was kept occupied,' he said.

44

Prison visits were remote and carefully guarded occasions

'Why had you thought there would be trouble in the Holy Land?'

'Because Noah Clark has taken over.' Arnold waved a fork with a potato speared on its prongs. 'And I suppose that means he's taken over Jake's forgery interests as well. So naturally I expect trouble. Jake will want to take it all back.'

'But there was no trouble?'

'None at all. Noah Clark slipped away before three o'clock, and that was all until the fire broke out.'

'How did the fire begin?'

Arnold laughed. 'Who knows how fires are started? Oil lamps fall over, and old rags smoulder for hours before flaring up. I don't know. The chief fireman said it was caused by some new fangled printing equipment, although Jem Catnach's printing works is next door. Moses Arenson runs a sweat shop.'

'What do you mean?'

'I mean that the fireman was probably mistaken. There wasn't any printing equipment there.'

Edith continued eating in silence for nearly a minute. Then she spoke. 'If the problem for forgers of paper money is the heavy new electrical equipment, then doesn't it follow that next door to a printer's factory would be the

45

best place to install it? It would look as if new machinery was intended for Mr Catnach, and nobody would give it a second thought.' She frowned in slight disapproval as Arnold wiped the gravy from his plate with a piece of bread. 'I wonder whether Mr Arenson's sweat shop is the headquarters of your forgery ring?'

'Clever,' Arnold said slowly. 'Very clever. My goodness!'

'In which case, the fact that Mr Arenson might have been burned to death and the sweat shop destroyed could mean that the Holy Land wasn't as quiet last night as you thought.'

'My goodness, Edith,' he said in admiration, 'it's you who should have been the policeman!'

She smiled happily, and went to fetch the roly-poly pudding.

4. *EVENING*

At a quarter to nine Arnold Pipkin was waiting on parade in the yard behind Bow Street police station. There were seventy men lined up in sections, rigidly to attention behind the nine sergeants. It was not quite dark, but the two street lamps in the square cast a gloomy pattern of shadows against the ground.

'I hears you're going hunting tonight, Arnold,' 325 P.C. O'Donnell whispered.

'That's right,' Arnold muttered.

'With Inspector Field of the Detectives and that busybody newspaperman?'

'I don't know anything about a newspaperman. There's a Mr Brennan from the Royal Mint. . . .'

'Silence in the ranks there!'

The door opened from the main building, and Inspector Drew marched on to the parade ground. He looked quite a small man in the dusk. He was followed by a wide awake Sergeant Green with the muster roll and the orderly book. They halted under the light from the window. 'Attention!' The sergeant from the head of each section stepped forward. 'Open order!' The roll was called. Six men were told to remain at the station in reserve for the night. Then came the serious business of the evening: Inspector Drew opened the Punishment Book.

P.C. James Paish, for being found in the tap room of the King Charles public house at half past midnight: fined two shillings.

P.C. Henry Evershed, for riding his horse at an improper speed and abusing his sergeant when spoken to when on mounted duty: severely reprimanded and cautioned.

Sergeant Philip Reader, for failing to report a burglary in Hart Street: suspended from duty for one month.

Then followed the list of missing persons, with age, height, build and colouring, which Arnold always found so confusing. Distinguishing characteristics were all right—a twisted finger on the left hand or a pronounced limp, and Arnold could bear the person in mind. But all these people of average build with light-dark complexions aged between twenty and forty-five would stay missing for ever as far as he was concerned. He was beginning to lose concentration by the time Inspector Drew reached the list of missing property. A horse was missing, and a cart, a brooch, a baby and a pound of butter.

At last, to ensure that the men were still awake, Inspector Drew inspected the ranks. It was his aim to see that the men had remembered their rattles and filled their lamps and were smartly turned out. He always sent the men on their way with a sermon about securely fastened doors, keeping carriages to their ranks and catching burglars. But on this particular evening Inspector Drew had a more solemn announcement to make. Their founder, the great Sir Robert Peel was dead.

'The whole nation has been thrust into mourning, and the House of Commons has adjourned in his honour. We must continue with our duties, aware as we are that we shall be his enduring monument. . . .' Drew talked of the politician's integrity and his love of the people, the sacrifices he had made for his country.

Arnold found himself moved, and during the two minutes silence he reflected on the grief of the people. He wondered what Edith would say. She had always been rather critical of the father of the modern police force: according to her the Peel family had bought their baronetcy by contributing £10 000 to Pitt's war with France. Grandfather Peel had exploited the new spinning jenny to transform himself from a humble calico printer into the richest cotton merchant in England, without paying a penny to the inventor. He had imported large numbers of pauper children into his factories from London. The family had become rich, but it had taken two generations to become respectable.

'A fair page in his country's history,' Drew was reciting, 'was the dearest object of Sir Robert Peel's life; and though we, his contemporaries, living amid the heat and dust of the conflicts in which he was engaged, are neither enabled nor entitled to speak for those who shall come after us, we do not run any great risk of committing an error when we assert that the unborn historian who shall write the full and impartial history of the first half of the nineteenth century in Great Britain will find in civil life no purer or higher reputation to identify with it than that of Sir Robert Peel.'

Arnold marched from the parade ground with a heavy feeling of patriotic sadness. As he broke ranks by the door and returned into the police station he unobtrusively brushed a tear from his cheek. He had to admit that Inspector Drew could rise to the occasion when required.

The six reserve constables filed into the general office. Arnold ambled in behind them. 'Did you know that the Bow Street Runners saved Sir Robert Peel from being killed in a duel?' Arnold asked them. 'When he was Home

Sir Robert Peel died on 2 July 1850

Secretary, that was, and he made sure the Runners stepped in to prevent the duel. . . .' From the icy reception Arnold deduced that the moment for his anecdote was ill-timed.

The constables who had come off duty at nine o'clock were beginning to report in. The routine of the night was already established. Sergeant Westgate was interviewing a lushington, as drunks were called, who had been celebrating his fiftieth birthday too enthusiastically. 'Have you anything about your person you would like me to take care of?' asked the Sergeant. They were not allowed to search a man unless he was suspected of a crime, so they asked him instead whether he wanted anything taken care of. The Sergeant gestured P.C. Evans to go through the lushington's pockets.

Arnold sat in the wooden armchair and made an entry in his pocket book to account for the previous night's extra money. 'Assisted with the fire escape, received one shilling. . . .' The rest of the men watched the search with professional indifference.

'Jailer!' Sergeant Westgate called eventually. 'Take him away to the cells!'

At half past nine the raiding party assembled. Inspector Field and three of his men arrived, furtively whispering and walking with exaggerated caution so that every constable in the station looked up to stare. They found that Mr Brennan was already there, standing unobtrusively at the desk reading the week's *Police Gazette*. And then the fashionable newspaperman arrived.

'I don't know why he's coming with us,' Arnold complained to Sergeant Westgate. 'He'll be waylaid and robbed.'

'Not with you to look after him, Ninety-four.' And besides, Sergeant Westgate thought it was a good idea for the public to know what the police had to cope with.

'They wouldn't allow Mr Mayhew to interview us,' Arnold grumbled.

'Mr Mayhew wasn't a personal friend of Inspector Field,' he said with a grin.

Arnold was then called in for the briefing session. This was a detective raid, and Arnold was there to give assistance. He was not to interfere or obstruct, and he should take his orders from Inspector Field. As soon as the raid was successfully accomplished Arnold was to return to his beat.

'Yes, sir,' said Arnold. He glanced nervously at the fashionable newspaperman, who seemed to be writing things down in a notebook. 'By the way, I've been thinking about the printing press. . . .'

'Leave the thinking to me, Constable,' said Inspector Field with a tap of his nose. 'It's your job to take us as unobtrusively as possible to Dudley Street and get us into the lodging house. We'll take them entirely by surprise. Some of my men will guard the rear in Cat Alley to prevent escape.'

'Yes,' said Arnold. 'But I think the printing. . . .'

'We shall need speed once the operation starts. The Holy Land is like all these rookeries, it has secret cellars and passageways and roads across the rooftops. If they see us coming they'll be six streets away.'

Inspector Field led his party from the station. As they left they saw a plate of cold pork and thick slices of bread and butter being taken in on a tray with a small bottle of brandy for Inspector Drew's evening meal. They crept noisily off into the night.

Field seemed to know the bars and gin shops and stall holders nearly as

Emigrants waiting on the dockside at Cork, driven by poverty to England and America in their thousands

well as Arnold knew them, and he stopped frequently to recall the good old days when he had sent this man off to Newgate for three years and that man away to the colonies for seven. He was a compulsive story teller, and all his stories showed up Inspector Field as a masterly and fearless detective since the day thirty years ago when he had joined the Bow Street Runners. They paused again when they reached Rose Street, while Inspector Field talked with a reformed burglar. The newspaperman turned to Arnold and enquired where he came from, and whether he missed the open countryside of Godalming.

'Well,' said Arnold, suddenly flattered, 'I can still enjoy the smells of the flowers and the vegetables, because I live with them here in the market.' The writer nodded his agreement. 'But I miss the grass and the sight of the trees. I'd like to go back there before I die.'

'Do you think you will?'

'I doubt it,' Arnold said sadly.

The newspaperman apparently worked from an office in Wellington Street off the Strand, so he knew Covent Garden well. But he hadn't ventured into the rookeries very often. 'In my early years,' he said to Arnold as they

Inside the Holy Land, where policemen seldom ventured alone

watched a heavily laden cart go by, 'when I had no money I took a turn in Covent Garden and stared at the pineapples in the market.'

'Those days would seem to be long past, sir,' Arnold observed.

'I hope so.' He looked distantly towards Trafalgar Square and Chandos Street, as if they held memories. 'I used to think this was a savage and wonderful district. It was full of colour and violence, but I have the impression people were happier then.'

Arnold nodded. 'There's no doubt of that, sir.' He had no idea whether the people had been happy a quarter of a century earlier, but he knew they were pretty miserable now. 'It was the famine that did it, sir. So many Irish came over here four years ago—they'll work for nothing and they live on less, so they've spoiled the prospects for the rest. There are more people starving in the rookeries now than ever before.'

The newspaperman agreed, and mentioned the decline in railway building as another factor that had hit the manual labourer. Not to mention the drop in food prices—since the repeal of the corn law the profit was so small that the costers and street traders were having a very difficult time.

'Yes,' said Arnold. 'People were happier twenty-five years ago.'

The raiding party had reached the Holy Land, and the inhabitants

The teeming poverty of the rookeries

seemed to have spilled out onto the streets as if the buildings were too crowded to take them all at once. The streets were running with sewage and filth the colour of green tea; it was swarming with flies and insects and infants. Arnold was so accustomed to it all that he was surprised at the reaction of the newspaperman, who was saying that the cholera epidemic of last year was entirely to be expected in such conditions.

Inspector Field was in the middle of a tale about a diamond pin and a race track gang, but Arnold was watching the newspaperman's face. He was observing the busy streets with fascination, taking in the sinister old men with bent bodies and mysterious sacks over their shoulders, the surly small urchins with clothes four sizes too large, or too small; he was peering at the ancient bow windows, the gas lamps, the waving flags of newly washed shirts and underwear that seemed to flutter from a thousand dingy windows.

The main, gaslit streets were narrow enough, but the side streets and back alleys were totally dark and gave the impression that the houses had fallen in upon each other to create dangerous passages through a network of cellars. The silence in these passageways was more menacing than the noisy lawlessness of the streets. Arnold shone his bullseye lantern into the darkness and saw the scurrying rats and urchins and beggars moving for cover.

'Is it far to Cat Alley?' asked the newspaperman.

'Not far, sir,' said Arnold. 'But we're approaching it from behind. If we go down Church Lane here. . . .'

A rowdy mob were gathered on the corner, shouting encouragement and arguing among themselves while two drunken women were fighting. The two women were scratching and kicking each other, and their screams of rage and pain were attracting people from all the surrounding streets.

'Excuse me, sir,' said Arnold, and he hurried across to the scene of the battle. 'Sarah! Sarah, stop this at once!' He pushed his way through the crowd. 'Mrs Sullivan, come here!' He grasped the two women and pulled them apart. 'Stop it, you hussies!'

There were boos and cries of disappointment from the spectators, and Sarah kicked Arnold in the ankle. 'Now now now,' said Arnold, 'we'll have no more of this. What will our distinguished visitors think of the Holy Land if they see this kind of behaviour?'

Arnold heard the whisper go round that that was Inspector Field over there; he was clearly well known to many of the men. Arnold gave the women a brief lecture on keeping the peace and tried to shoo the crowd away. The newspaperman was visibly shocked by what he had seen.

'What do the detectives want tonight?' asked one of the bystanders. 'Arnold doesn't usually come through here with detectives.'

'Didn't you know that Jake Sweeting's escaped from the Steel? Arnold is probably showing Mr Field where to find him.'

54

The smell of fish was pervasive in the rookeries

The three men with Inspector Field were in plain clothes, but the people of the Holy Land could recognise detective sergeants when they saw them. Arnold wondered whether they had ever taken anybody by surprise in their lives. Mr Brennan had been following a few yards behind all the way, and he too looked conspicuously like an agent of law and order.

'They'll never catch him!' said a voice in the crowd.

They went the next 200 yards in silence, and then when Arnold pointed to the narrow lane marked off with a heavy wooden barrier Inspector Field broke into a sudden run. They had reached Cat Alley. He gestured to his detective sergeants, this man at the barrier, Thornton down the other end of the alley and Smith round the back.

'Which house is it, Constable?' he hissed.

Arnold identified the block of three. The doors were broken and every window seemed to be filled with staring faces. The raid had become somewhat theatrical, especially since the crowd from Church Lane had followed to watch the fun. Somebody from across the street gave a piercing, warning whistle.

'Keep an eye on the rooftops,' Inspector Field commanded. He turned to Arnold. 'All right, Constable, lead the way.'

'This way, sir,' Arnold muttered. He dodged into the doorway of Jake Sweeting's lodging house. It was completely dark inside. 'We'll try the basement first,' he said. 'Unless he's seen us coming he should. . . .'

'He might be hiding,' said Mr Brennan.

'Of course he's hiding,' said Inspector Field. 'He's an escaped convict.' But he followed Arnold along the passage to the door leading down into the basement. Arnold picked out the way with his bullseye lantern, down the steps and along another passage. They stopped at a door at the end of the building.

'Open up!' called Mr Brennan. He hammered on the door. 'This is the Royal Mint!'

Inspector Field was less formal. 'I'm Inspector Field,' he called. 'Open this door before I smash it open!' He turned complacently to the newspaperman. 'They all know Charlie Field.' He waited for a moment, and then lifted his boot to the lock. It was an almighty kick, and the woodwork splintered into tiny pieces. 'After you, Constable.'

The room was clean and expensively furnished, filled with ornaments and bric-à-brac, flowers in glass domes and papier mâché chairs, heavy brocade draperies. Arnold was immediately and instinctively respectful. Mrs Sweeting was in command of the situation, standing with dignity in black satin beside Noah Clark, who was in his waistcoat and shirtsleeves by the fireplace.

Brennan scurried past Arnold in his eagerness to search the premises—the kitchen to the left, a bedroom beyond, looking quickly into the cupboards.

'Hello, Charlotte,' said the Inspector with menacing amiability. 'I thought you had a smart little place in Hampstead these days?'

She smiled icily. 'I've let the cottage to two young gentlemen for fifteen shillings a week. I prefer living here, where I belong. It's more neighbourly, most of the time.' She turned to the fashionable newspaperman. 'You don't look like an esclop, dearie. Did Charlie Field promise you an exciting night on the town? He always has had a weakness for mixing with the toffs. But there'll be no excitement here. I'm spending a peaceful evening at home with my husband.'

That seemed to be Noah Clark's cue to speak. 'Yea,' he growled, 'and who's going to pay for that door to be mended?'

'Don't worry, Mrs Sweeting,' Arnold said happily. 'If we find nothing here to incriminate you I'm sure the Detective Department will pay.'

Inspector Field glowered at Arnold and elbowed him to one side. 'Are you two people the registered occupants of these premises?' he demanded.

'We own the place, if that's what you mean,' said Noah Clark.

'You mean that I own the place,' said Mrs Sweeting.

'That's right. What do you think we are, burglars?'

Mr Brennan completed his search and came back looking disappointed. 'There's nothing here,' he said. 'No presses, chemicals or paper.' He glanced disbelievingly at Noah Clark. 'And there's no sign of the wanted man either.'

'What wanted man?' asked Noah. 'Ere, do you mind explaining something to me? What the 'ell's going on?'

Inspector Field sat in a plush, comfortable armchair. 'We're looking for Mr Sweeting.'

'What would he be doing here? We've taken over, haven't we? Jake wouldn't be welcome here, even if he came, and he knows it!'

'But he did come here,' said the Inspector. 'He came back last night.' He turned to the newspaperman. 'You see the loyalty of these people, sir? They have no natural instincts. Jake Sweeting was supposed to be this lady's husband, and she's chucked him for this little fellow.'

Charlotte snorted contemptuously. 'I'm loyal to myself, Charlie Field. If I had your natural instincts I'd have gone straight from the workhouse to Newgate prison. Do you mind leaving us now? Search the rest of the building if you like, and the houses next door. But leave us alone.'

Inspector Field had accepted defeat. 'All right, Charlotte,' he said wearily. 'But you'll still end up in Newgate. It isn't natural to refuse refuge to your husband.'

Charlotte laughed as they went off upstairs to search the rest of the lodging house.

'Aren't we going to arrest anybody?' the newspaperman asked anxiously.

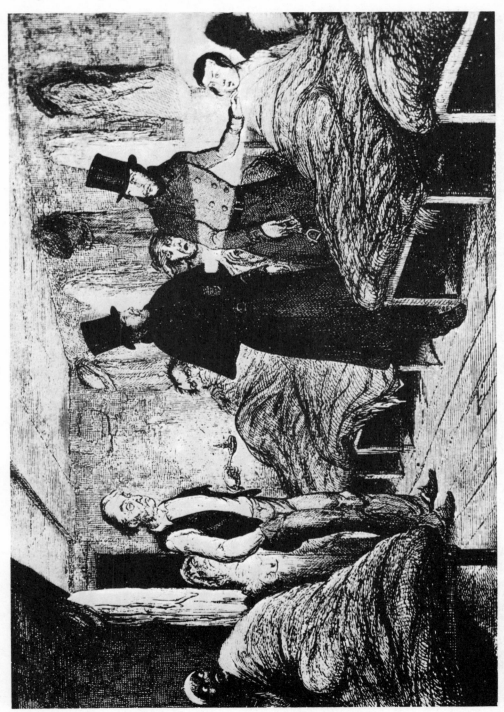

Taken by the police in a threepenny lodging house

'We've nothing against them, sir,' said Inspector Field. 'It's no offence just to be a criminal.' He began the tour, disturbing people sleeping eight and ten in a room, stepping over cursing bodies, shining his lantern on a muddle of humanity. It was going to be a long and purposeless search. Arnold padded off the end of the alley and summoned Sergeant Thornton. 'We didn't find him,' he said. He went off to the other end of the alley, to Dudley Street. 'Come on,' he said to the detective. 'We're going through the entire place.'

'No luck, no printing presses, no escaped convict?'

'Of course not,' said Arnold. 'They've been operating from Monmouth Court, haven't they? I keep on trying to tell that inspector of yours, they've been using that sweat shop in Monmouth Court, the one that was burned down last night.'

'Oh well, as long as nobody was killed.' He strode on ahead of Arnold. 'What I always say is that if you're still alive then you haven't much to complain about.'

'But somebody was burned to death.'

The detective had gone into the lodging house and begun his search. Arnold could hear the man calling out, 'All right, this is an identity parade. Everybody stand by your beds!' Arnold shrugged his shoulders and went back to find Inspector Field.

After forty-five minutes they had arrested two pickpockets and a drunk, as well as a woman who had attacked Inspector Field for shining his lantern in her face. It was, Field assured the newspaperman, a reasonable haul for one night. They trudged off back to Bow Street, leaving Arnold to return to his beat.

'Good night,' the newspaperman said to Arnold. 'I'm grateful to you for sparing the time.' Apparently the man had written several books. Arnold decided to ask Edith about them. She was always reading books, and she would know all about the man.

Crunch, crunch, crunch, along West Street.

'Evening, Mr Pipkin,' said Oliver the Pieman. 'Feeling hungry?'

Arnold groaned. 'I'd need to be starving. . . .' The pies were probably filled with catsmeat, or three-week-old rabbit. Piemen were a disappearing breed now, since Sweeny Todd had made people suspicious. Poor old Oliver was finding it hard to continue. 'I'll toss you for it,' said Arnold.

He took a penny from his pocket. 'Call.' The pieman called tails and the penny came down heads. Arnold put the penny back in his pocket and took a hot pie. It smelled quite appetising, but Arnold was fussy about his food. 'Here,' he called to a street urchin who was staring hungrily. 'Do you want a pie?'

The urchin snatched it with disbelief. 'Cor,' he said, 'thanks, Mr Pipkin.' He scurried away with the pie before Arnold could change his mind.

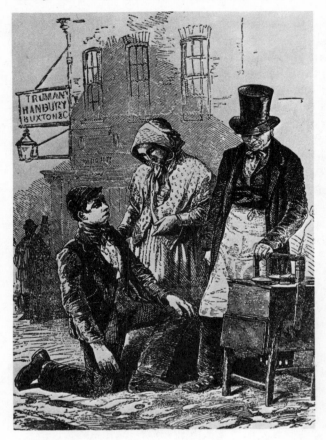

Tossing the pieman

'I spy blue, I spy black,' the urchin's voice rang out defiantly, 'I spy a peeler in a shiny hat.'

Arnold continued round his beat. Number four beat of Section One, E Division, along both sides of Little St Andrew Street from Seven Dials to West Street, with the side of West Street and both sides of Little Earl Street back to the Seven Dials, including Tower Street, Lumber Court and Monmouth Court. He paused at Monmouth Court to stare at the ruins of Moses Arenson's sweat shop.

'There's not much of it left now, is there, Mr Pipkin?'

It was Kit Oldcastle, lurking about in the shadows as always. Arnold shook his head. There was only a pile of rubble and mud and the smell of burnt timber.

'I hear you came to the station yesterday morning,' said Arnold. 'You wanted to tell me about the corpse that was found.' It was half past eleven,

60

time for one of Arnold's routine calls. 'Let me buy you a drink, Kit. You've earned it.'

The tap room of the Spencer's Arms was half empty; there were only the usual derelicts with nowhere else to go, a couple of drunks and some men discussing the Saturday night dog fight. They took little notice of Arnold. His usual tankard was already on the counter waiting for him.

'Evening, Mr Paul,' he said officially. 'Everything as it should be tonight?'

'Yes, thank you, Mr Pipkin. Have this on the house.'

'Well well, that's uncommon kind.' Arnold bought half a pint of stout for the old man, then he went and sat by the window. 'Good health,' he murmured to Kit Oldcastle. He drank appreciatively. 'I needed that,' he said with a sigh. 'I've spent the whole evening with the Detective Force, getting thirstier and thirstier, running in and out of those lodging houses, and all for what?'

'For nothing,' Kit Oldcastle agreed.

'I tried to tell them that the forgery was being conducted from here, but they wouldn't listen. They could have examined the ruins and found out how the fire started. They might even have found a burnt-out printing press.'

Kit Oldcastle gave a cautious bob of the head. 'The firemen did find a burnt-out printing press in the yard. But it was badly damaged—probably an old one belonging to Jem Catnach. That's what everybody thought.'

'Naturally.' The yard at the back ran along behind the printing factory, Moses Arenson's place and the butcher's shop. 'And what does everybody think about the body, Kit? Who do they think died last night?'

Kit looked at his empty glass. 'I'll have a large one this time, Mr Pipkin.'

Arnold bought him another drink. He could guess what everybody was thinking. That Jake Sweeting had come back to claim his property, his printing press and his blocks and paper, that Jake had been hiding out in the sweat shop when it caught fire. But it would be nice to know that he guessed correctly.

'I did hear that Jake was seen,' Kit Oldcastle said, 'going into the building last night. But it's only gossip, you understand, Mr Pipkin, probably no more true than the story that Noah Clark was having the sweat shop watched all evening.' Kit laughed. 'After all, you would have seen if anything unusual was going on, wouldn't you?'

'Of course.' Arnold thought for a moment. He had seen Amy Hill lurking about in Monmouth Court; he had seen Noah Clark creeping off into the night. Had Amy been keeping watch for Jake's arrival? And had Noah been told when Jake had gone into the sweat shop? But surely Noah would not have burnt the place to the ground!

'Well, people like to speculate,' said Kit. 'Who will ever know what really happened?'

'What about Moses Arenson?' asked Arnold. 'Couldn't the dead body be him?'

'Moses? I thought you said he'd run away to Birmingham till this was over? Moses always did know when to stay out of the way.'

'You're a villain, Kit Oldcastle,' said Arnold. He wiped his mouth with the back of his hand, put his top hat back on straight and glowered down at the man. 'I wouldn't be surprised if it wasn't *you* who kept watch for Jake Sweeting's return.'

'Who, me, Mr Pipkin? But we were speculating, that was all.'

The empty streets could be boring—this engraving shows the slightly different uniform and the more modern helmet which were introduced in 1867

Mm, that was all. Arnold called good night to Mr Paul and left. They were all villains. What was the point of trying to look after them? They were all completely indifferent to the law, and none of them appreciated what Arnold tried to do for them.

The clock on St Giles' Church struck twelve as Arnold resumed his beat. He felt better now. There was nothing like a tankard of stout to help a policeman through the long night. He tucked his fingers into his belt and walked away.

5. *THE NATIONAL SCENE*

On Tuesday, 29 September 1829, 3000 newly created 'peelers' had marched onto the streets of London to commence their duties. The force was under Mr Richard Mayne, a brilliant young lawyer, and Colonel Charles Rowan, an army officer who had served with distinction at Waterloo. They had their headquarters at the old Whitehall Palace overlooking Scotland Yard. Seventeen divisions had been formed, each with about 165 men under a superintendent. Each superintendent was in command of four inspectors, who were in command of four sergeants.

The creation of a police force had been considered necessary for many years, and the changes in society after the Industrial Revolution made the need even more pressing. The social causes of disorder were worsening: the population had been growing rapidly, the towns were becoming overcrowded, and there was massive unemployment in both towns and rural areas. The slums had grown in size and the quality of life was grim. Violence and crime were as inevitable as hunger, and the cheapest way to escape from this unbearable reality was provided by gin.

The mob had become a significant threat to political and economic stability, and when the mob rioted, as it frequently did, the army was used to restore order. Parliament, of course, did not take kindly to these activities, but it took nearly fifty years to pass an Act designed to cope with the problem of riots. Between 1780 and 1829 there were seventeen committees set up to investigate the whole question of maintaining law. The sixteenth of these was set up in 1816 and it reported back to Parliament in 1820. Its Report was published in 1822, and its main recommendation was that there should be a single police force for the whole of London.

To understand how sensitive a political issue this was, we must bear in mind that the French Revolution was still vivid in people's memory, that the French gendarmes were considered to be a threat to civil liberty, and that the use of the British army to put down riots invariably gave rise to public outcry. A new police force, it had been thought, would merely increase the power of the State.

Sir Robert Peel's Metropolitan Police Act was passed, however, with very little opposition in Parliament. But in provincial towns the old system of constables and the watch continued.

64

The National Scene

The mounted police in the eighteenth century

The river police around 1900

The Watch house, Bow Street in 1812

In 1834 Liverpool was known as 'the black spot of the Mersey'; with a population of nearly a quarter of a million it retained only fifty watchmen to keep order. Portsmouth had a population of 50 000 with only twenty-two constables and watch to keep order. Hull was one of the few towns to have a police force, crudely modelled on the Bow Street Runners, and its population of 39 000 was looked after by a Chief Constable with thirty-nine men, who were paid when they made an arrest; their motto was 'no prisoner, no pay'. And these were the most unruly, seaport cities.

66

A hand ambulance which was used between 1860 and 1938, very useful for drunks and brawlers

The situation was improved by the 1835 Municipal Corporations Act, which required the 178 boroughs to which it applied to appoint a watch committee who were to create a police force sufficient to maintain order in the borough *and* its surrounding area.

In 1836 a Royal Commission was appointed to consider the problem of a rural police force, and this commission reported in 1839. Whilst the government was brooding over the recommendations the first serious outbreak of Chartist disorders occurred. There were numerous local strikes, there was rioting in London and Birmingham, and twenty-four men were killed by the army in Newport. The government were, consequently, spurred into action. Justices were *enabled* to maintain a paid police force for the whole or part of their counties. The number of policemen was not to exceed one for every 1000 inhabitants, and the cost was to be borne from the local rates.

The results were disappointing, mainly because local authorities were aware that Peel's metropolitan force had been paid for by a levy on the parish rate of 8d in the pound. So by 1856 there were police forces in only twenty-four counties and in parts of seven more. Twenty counties had no police force whatever. In consequence, the County and Borough Police Act of 1856 *required* the justices to establish a paid police force for the whole of each county. However, it provided for the government to pay twenty-five per cent of the cost of pay and clothing (this assistance was increased in 1888 to fifty per cent).

The Act also created Crown Inspectors of Constabulary, who were to visit county and borough forces and report on their efficiency to the Home Secretary. This efficiency improved markedly throughout the Victorian era. The Inspectors reported:

120 forces inefficient in 1857
78 forces inefficient in 1860
56 forces inefficient in 1870
38 forces inefficient in 1875
25 forces inefficient in 1885
no forces inefficient in 1890

Commentators have always been inclined to think that the efficiency of the police would be achieved only by creating a single police force under direct Home Office control. In 1857 there were 239 police forces, some consisting only of a handful of men and ranging to the Metropolitan force of 6640 men; they were appointed and controlled in varying ways, and their methods of operation were inclined to differ. The critics derived satisfaction from the fact that in 1900 the number of forces had been slightly reduced to 197. But there was still no uniformly applied police system, and there is none today.

A better index of police efficiency is the ratio of policemen to population, and this also improved throughout the Victorian era:

Year	Number of Provincial Policemen	Number of London Policemen	Inhabitants per Officer Provinces	London
1830	—	3 350	—	455
1840	—	4 840	—	443
1857	12 000	6 640	1 365	446
1861	13 000	7 230	1 300	441
1871	15 860	10 350	1 187	375
1881	19 480	12 020	1 091	402
1891	23 070	15 890	1 014	355
1901	27 360	16 900	949	396

Of course, numbers are not the sole criterion for an effective police force. It will be remembered that Fielding selected only six men to be trained as the first Bow Street Runners, and these formed the nucleus of what became a

The Bow Street Office, early in the nineteenth century

Scotland Yard, the headquarters of the metropolitan police until 1888

highly efficient detective force. The Bow Street Runners continued as a detective force after 1829, but no new men were appointed and they became virtually extinct within ten years. And the 'peelers' were not detectives, they were men on the beat, their job was mainly the *prevention* of crime. So periodically, when a particularly bloody murder occurred, the new police could look a little inadequate.

Such a murder occurred in 1842. The police visited the Roehampton home of an Irish coachman called Daniel Good to question him about a shoplifting charge, but this was quickly forgotten when they found a woman's dismembered body in his harness room. There was a bloodstained axe in the corner, and Good had clearly been trying to burn the woman's head in the fireplace. While the police were examining this room Good locked them in and fled.

Gradually the police put together a case against Good; they learned that the dead woman was Jane Jones and that she had lived with Good as his wife in Manchester Square. When Good had gone to Roehampton he had left Jane Jones and taken up with another woman called Lydia Butcher. Lydia Butcher had become pregnant. The clinching evidence against Good was his story to neighbours in Manchester Square that 'Mrs Good' had left because she had found 'a place', whereas Good had taken away many of her posses-sions and had given Lydia Butcher a bonnet and shawl belonging to his wife. But the police had no idea where Good had gone, and it took several weeks to find him by pure accident, working as a bricklayer in Tonbridge.

In response to the public concern the Commissioners of Police set up a small detective force at the metropolitan headquarters in Scotland Yard. The new force consisted of two inspectors and six sergeants; their operations were mainly confined to London, although like the Bow Street Runners they were available to assist in provincial investigations if their help were requested.

There was a revival of the familiar argument about the danger of a police state, especially since the new force would wear plain clothes and might act as agents provocateurs. In 1845 the argument against the Detective Force was still continuing in *Punch*:

> Its (the force's) members, disguised in plain clothes, are now known to mix in all societies, to whose manners and peculiarities they are instructed to adapt themselves. They mingle, as exquisites, in the 'salons' of fashion; they creep, as cads, into the 'crib' of the costermonger. They frequent every species of tavern, from the first rate to the Jerry-shop; and neither the freedom of the tap nor the sanctity of the parlour is safe from their intrusion. . . . But the evil does not stop here. In his uniform the Policeman is notorious for scraping acquaintances with servants at area railings . . . How much longer are free born Englishmen to submit to the espionage and to be vistimised by the voracity of an X10, a Y15 or a Z20?

The first case in which the Detective Force lent assistance was in Rode, a small Somerset village. There a factory inspector called Samuel Kent had married his housekeeper; he had two children by a previous marriage and the housekeeper had one. The housekeeper's child was murdered. Scotland Yard sent down Inspector Jonathan Whicher and Sergeant Adolphus Williamson. The Inspector was soon convinced that the child had been killed by his step-sister Constance. But the Inspector was too hasty; he arrested her on insufficient evidence, and Constance was soon released. The press created a massive weight of public opinion against Inspector Whicher and he was forced to resign. The young Sergeant Williamson did not resign, and a few years later when Constance entered a convent and then confessed to the murder it was he—by now Inspector Williamson—who arrested her. Williamson became head of the Detective Department in 1869.

If the early years of the Detective Force were less than a total triumph there was worse to come in 1876. This was when a man called Hugh Mont-gomery organised a racing fraud. He printed a fake newspaper called *The Sport*, in which there were stories of his success as a punter and the refusal of

English bookmakers to accept his bets. Montgomery used to send a copy of the newspaper to rich prospects, with a request that he or she should place a bet for him.

He asked the Comtesse de Goncourt to place a bet of £200 for him, and enclosed a cheque on the Royal Bank of London which was postdated for three months to satisfy, he claimed, British currency regulations. The horse allegedly won and the Comtesse received 5 per cent commission. She was impressed, and the next time it happened she added £10 000 of her own money to the bet. Then she tried to raise £30 000 for a bet. Her solicitors became suspicious and decided to investigate. They found that the firm of bookmakers she was using did not exist, that the horses she was backing did not exist, there was no such bank as the Royal Bank of London and there were no such currency regulations as Montgomery claimed.

The cheque for £10 000 had been cashed, however. The Detective Force was called in, and Chief Inspector Druscovitch was sent to arrest Mr Montgomery. Druscovitch was too late: Montgomery had flown. But the Chief Inspector did discover that the £10 000 had been cashed into Scottish Clydesdale Bank notes by a cripple with scars on his face. He also found that the Scottish police were investigating an identical swindle, and had traced their gang to the Queen's Hotel, Bridge of Allan. Chief Inspector Druscovitch hurried away to Scotland with warrants for their arrest, but again the gang had just left.

In their rooms at the Queen's Hotel the Chief Inspector found letters and telegrams advising the gang of his own movements—these were in the handwriting of his colleague, Chief Inspector Palmer.

Superintendent Adolphus Williamson took over at once. He received a report that the gang were in Rotterdam and had paid their hotel bill with Clydesdale banknotes. Williamson went to Rotterdam, and he was extremely lucky to find that the men were still in custody. The Dutch police had received a telegram from Scotland Yard saying there had been a mistake and the gang were to be released, 'letter follows'. The Dutch police were waiting for the letter of confirmation.

Some of the gang members turned Queen's evidence and claimed that they had paid large bribes to Palmer, Druscovitch and the third of the Detective Force's chief inspectors, called Clarke. At the subsequent trial Palmer and Druscovitch were found guilty of corruption. Chief Inspector Clarke was acquitted, but he retired from the force and left Williamson without any chief inspectors.

A complete reorganisation was obviously needed; the Home Office responded by setting up an enquiry, and the name of the Detective Force was changed to the Criminal Investigation Department. A barrister named Howard Vincent served the committee of enquiry, and for them he made a detailed study of the French detective system. The committee decided on changes which they considered necessary, and these included the appointment of a Director of C.I.D. Howard Vincent applied for the job, and got it. Vincent set up the Criminal Records Office, appointed C.I.D. inspectors with a staff of sergeants for each metropolitan division, increased his establishment to some 800 men, and tightened his control over the department. Superintendent Williamson became a Chief Constable.

The new Director made several innovations which affected the wider police force. First he made improvements to the *Police Gazette*, altering its layout and introducing illustrations. Second, and more important, he was instrumental in producing a handbook, *The Police Code and Manual of the Criminal Law*. This gave a brief description of every criminal offence in alphabetical order, and was small enough to be carried in the pocket.

Prior to this a policeman's training in law was extremely sketchy, which put him at a disadvantage in court. Recruits had to be able to read and write, they had to be five feet eight inches tall, and they had to be recommended by a minister or other responsible person. Once accepted, they seem to have picked up the job as they went along. This may have been because even the most basic forms of training were unpopular with the men. *The Standard Newspaper* on Thursday, 25 September 1829 described the reaction of some early recruits to physical training:

> On Wednesday morning several divisions of the New Policemen were conducted through their alloted divisions by the different inspectors preparatory to their commencing permanent duty. On the following morning (yesterday) Herring, the Inspector of the 2nd Division, received no less a number than 28 resignations from among the newly appointed men in his division.
>
> It would appear that the new candidates for protecting the lives and property of H.M. subjects were not sufficiently aware what it was expected they should perform until they had gone through the initiatory drillings, the first of which caused so many resignations.

The drillings continued. In 1839 a Candidates' Preparatory Class was set up at Wellington Barracks, where a course of foot drill and firearms was supervised by a police sergeant. Howard Vincent's pocket book was the first recognition that a policeman might need a special educational training, and it was not until the 1930s that a special police college was actually created.

Shortly before his retirement Howard Vincent created the Special Branch. It had been during Sir Robert Peel's period of office as Secretary for Ireland that a prototype of the new police force was established to cope with the problems in Ireland. Now, sixty years later, the problems were spreading to

England, and there were bomb attacks by the Fenians in London. A tentative start had been made by the Fenians in 1867, when a Clerkenwell street was wrecked in an attempt to get Irish prisoners out of gaol. Twelve people were killed and 120 injured. But the real campaign to achieve Irish independence was launched in 1883, with simultaneous attacks on the government offices in King Charles Street and on *The Times* offices. In October the same year there were two more simultaneous attacks on the underground railway between Charing Cross and Westminster, and at Paddington. Nearly seventy people were injured at Paddington.

A Special Irish Branch of the police was set up, to guard public buildings and hunt out the bomb manufacturers. The Fenians responded by simultaneously trying to blow up Nelson's column and Scotland Yard. Nelson's column survived intact, but Scotland Yard was severely damaged. The Special Irish Branch were successful in arresting numerous terrorists, but the attacks continued into 1884, against railway stations and such symbolic objectives as London Bridge, the Tower of London and the House of Commons. Then the raids mysteriously ceased, and the word Irish was dropped from the Special Branch title.

Because of this expansion in Scotland Yard activity, and because the building itself had been damaged, new premises were designed by Norman Shaw and were built nearby with convict labour. The metropolitan police headquarters moved to New Scotland Yard in 1888.

The intervention of police force when political means had failed was not confined to the Irish problems; much of the historical necessity for the police arose from economic depression, starvation, homelessness and unemployment, even from the search for religious and social freedom. There was a direct connection between the first Chartist disorders and the 1839 County Police Enabling Act. There were more riots and industrial strikes in 1842, and more Chartist leaders were transported.

In 1848 the government, with a nervous eye on European revolutions, thought itself seriously threatened by the Chartists. It will be remembered that the 1838 People's Charter made six demands—for universal male suffrage, annual parliaments, equal electoral districts, the removal of property qualifications for Members of Parliament, payment of Members of Parliament, and a secret ballot. The leaders collected signatures and took them to Westminster for presentation to Parliament. The petition weighed over 5 cwt and was carried in three cabs.

It was not the petition, but the mob, which the government feared. The Chartist leaders were gathering their supporters on Kennington Common, and after the speeches they would all march through the streets to Westminster. Incredibly, 170 000 special constables were sworn in for the occasion. But no revolution was attempted.

New Scotland Yard became the new headquarters of the metropolitan police in 1888

'In the morning,' Charles Greville recorded in his memoirs, 'everybody was on the alert, the parks were closed; our office was fortified, a barricade of Council Registers was erected in the accessible room on the ground floor, and all our guns were taken down to be used in defence of the building. However, at about twelve o'clock crowds came streaming along Whitehall, going northwards, and it was announced that all was over. The intended tragedy was rapidly changed into a ludicrous farce. The Chartists, about 20 000 in number, assembled on Kennington Common. Presently Mr Mayne (Commissioner of Police) appeared on the ground, and sent one of his inspectors to say he wanted to speak to Feargus O'Connor to inform him that the meeting would not be interfered with, but the procession would not be allowed. Feargus insisted on shaking hands with Mr Mayne, swore he was his best of friends, and instantly harangued his rabble, advising them not to provoke a collision, and to go away quietly—advice they instantly obeyed, and with great alacrity and good humour. Thus all evaporated in smoke. The petition was brought down piecemeal and presented in the afternoon. Since that there has been an exposure of the petition itself, covering the authors of it with ridicule and disgrace. It turns out to be signed by less than two millions, instead of six as Feargus stated; and of those, there were no end of fictitious names, together with the insertion of every species of ribaldry, indecency and impertinence.'

A similar situation in 1833 was handled badly by the nervous authorities and had led to tragedy. The National Political Union of Working People had arranged a meeting in Calthorpe Street, behind Cold Bath Fields Prison, and the authorities were expecting trouble. They proclaimed the meeting illegal, and so attracted thousands of sightseers to watch the excitement. The police were ordered to break up the meeting at the first sign of trouble and to arrest the leaders.

Two thousand police attended the meeting, and the Home Secretary, Lord Melbourne, the two Commissioners of Police and a handful of magistrates, established themselves in a nearby public house to await developments. These began slowly. First a young union official called Lee arrived and made a speech to the crowd, then another official turned up and made a second speech. Eventually the members of the National Political Union of Working People arrived in procession, 150 men with banners and slogans. The police panicked and attacked the procession. Violent fighting broke out, many people were injured and a policeman called Cully was stabbed to death. Union officials were arrested, and the man who had stabbed Cully was tried for murder.

The verdict of the jury was unexpected.

> We find a verdict of justifiable homicide on these grounds: that no riot act was read, nor any proclamation advising the people to disperse, that the Government did not take the proper precautions to prevent the meeting from assembling, and that the conduct of the Police was ferocious, brutal and unprovoked by the people; and we moreover express our anxious hope that the Government will in future take better precautions to prevent a recurrence of such disgraceful transactions in the Metropolis.

This verdict was reversed by the court of appeal, and a committee of enquiry was set up, which found that the police had been acting according to instructions from Lord Melbourne or the Commissioner, Colonel Rowan, who blamed each other.

The jury's verdict must be seen in the context of a widespread hostility to the police; after the trial each member received a commemorative medal and became something of a hero. Although it is clear that the police were at fault, they were, however, expressing the will of the State against a popular movement, and it can be argued that this is one of their functions. Towards the end of the Victorian era such big demonstrations had become less against the constitution and more directly for industrial reasons. The Dockers' Tanner strike caused popular unrest in 1889. Bloody Sunday in 1887 was caused by mass unemployment; a huge demonstration in Trafalgar Square was dispersed by police and Life Guards, ten people were killed and more than a hundred injured.

The futility of trying to change society by fighting the police was nicely expressed by Bernard Shaw, who was proud of his reputation as the first man to run from Trafalgar Square on Bloody Sunday. 'He was sometimes reminded by the more pugnacious comrades that mobs do not always run away,' Hesketh Pearson records.

> On such occasions Shaw would reply by asserting that the French monarchy could have crushed the revolution if it had not been foolish enough to believe that Marie Antoinette's gambling debts were more important than the wages of its soldiers, who did not fraternise with the mob until their pay was four years in arrear. The pay of a London police constable in 1887 was only twenty-four shillings a week; but it was never in arrear, and the pension was certain. Consequently, though the constables were all proletarians, not one of them ever fraternised with the people or hesitated to knock them about or do their worst against them in the magistrates' courts. It was true, he admitted, that though insurgent mobs began by running away, the defeat and humiliation started in them a sullen rage which, if the provocation continued long enough, made them murderous, destructive, even fearless. He had felt the beginnings of it in himself. But what good would their destructiveness do them? If they murdered the police they destroyed their own security. If the burnt houses they would burn palaces and mansions instead of burning their own wretched slums. . . .

The police had, in fact, become very powerful defenders of the State by the end of the century. It could be argued that the State had its faults or that laws should be changed, but the police were doing an effective job in maintaining order. How the unemployed, or Bernard Shaw, should bring about their changes is a separate question, and has little to do with the *enforcement* of laws.

It must not be forgotten that the Victorians had been far from complacent about their society: the Chartists and the trade unionists, Sir Robert Peel

Covent Garden was a convenient place for political meetings

and Parliament, Dickens, Mayhew and the proud middle classes, even Adolphus Williamson and Arnold Pipkin—they were all fully aware of the imperfections of their society and took active steps—great or small according to their position—to bring about improvements. The Victorians were, in their way, humanitarians, and we must remember that many of the most harrowing accounts of cruelty and injustice were written by propagandists who shared our horror and had the full support of a massive public; Dickens was never persecuted as Cobbet had been for his literary activities. There is every reason to suppose that the majority of ordinary people were well in advance of the legislature.

When some English Jacobins were being held without trial in Cold Bath Fields prison, and being kept like most of the other prisoners on the verge of starvation, they managed to smuggle out a note written in their own blood with a splinter of wood on the flyleaf of a book, and this protesting note reached the attention of Sir Francis Burdett, a radical Member of Parliament. Burdett raised the matter in the House of Commons, and in 1800 a committee of enquiry was set up. Sir Francis Burdett became the hero of the London populace; when he stood for Parliament against a friend of the prison governor the campaign became centred upon prison conditions. Cobbett—who was still at that time a Tory—found the campaign distressing:

> The road from Piccadilly to the hustings at Brentford is a scene of confusion and sedition, such as never was beheld, except in the environs of Paris, during the most dreadful times of the revolution . . . The road . . . is lined with ragged wretches from St Giles' bawling out 'Sir Francis Burdett and No Bastille' and at the hustings there are daily some half a dozen convicts who have served their time in the house of correction, employed in amusing the rabble with execrations on the head of Mr Mainwaring.

Sir Francis won the election, but the result was reversed on a technicality about the time the polls closed; a few years later Sir Francis returned to Parliament, this time with Cobbett's ardent support. The tide of radicalism had turned.

The committee of enquiry reported that some abuses did exist at Cold Bath Fields prison; so a special commission was appointed to look into the findings of the report, and this special committee decided that there were no abuses.

> It appears to your committee, that the sherriff has been imposed upon, and that the statement made to him originated in misapprehension, and was altogether frivolous and unfounded. And your said committee lastly report, that they have frequently examined into the state and condition

The freeing of prisoners, Cold Bath Fields

The Water Engine,
Cold Bath Fields Prison

of the house of correction, and of the several prisoners there confined; they have found the prison perfectly clean, and the prisoners healthy and without complaint: and your committee have great satisfaction in representing to the House that it appears to them, by the information of the Rev. Mr Evans, the chaplain to the prison, and Mr Aris, the governor, that the prisoners behave orderly, with decency and due decorum in the chapel during divine service; and that the children, who are kept separate and apart from their parents, make great progress in their learning.

Cold Bath Fields prison was said to have been planned and conducted 'on the principles of the late benevolent Mr Howard'. There were 333 cells in the prison, plus some larger apartments for those who could afford to pay half a guinea a week for them. 'The prison is divided into two sides, the male and the female,' as described by Rudolph Ackermann. 'On the male side are five day rooms for the convicts, two rooms for the vagrants, who are sent there for seven days previous to their being passed to their respective parishes; one separate apartment for the debtors, one infirmary, one foul ward, and an apartment for the clerks. On the female side are six day rooms, a wash house, two store rooms, one infirmary, one foul ward, and an apartment for the children of the convicts, who are kept separate from their parents, and are taught to read, say their catechism, etc.; they have three meals a day, and are comfortably clothed.' The adult prisoners were employed in useful labour.

Cold Bath Fields prison was built around 1793, and so it benefited from some of the reforms which such people as Howard had been advocating. Between November 1793 and November 1807 there had been 19 862 prisoners there; and it was claimed in support of the prison conditions that only ninety-one had died there, whilst twenty-four had, in fact, been born there.

John Howard had been the Sherriff of Bedfordshire; in 1773 he had written a book, *The State of Prisons*, and the first step which he wanted to see taken was for prisons to be controlled by local authorities instead of private enterprise. He died in 1790, when Elizabeth Fry was ten years old. Elizabeth Fry became best known for her work in Newgate prison, where she used to read the Bible to the prisoners. She held that cruel punishments were no deterrent to crime but were likely to turn criminals into hardened criminals. She wanted young prisoners and first offenders kept separate from the old lags, women kept separate from men, the system to be geared to reformation and rehabilitation, and of course she wanted better conditions. She was especially concerned for the women, claiming that twelve hours on the treadmill did little for the female character.

Elizabeth Fry visited prisons throughout the country, and was associated with John Gurney and Thomas Fowell Buxton (her brother-in-law, who wrote *An Enquiry whether Crime and Misery are Produced or Prevented by our Present System of Prison Discipline*) and she gave evidence to at least one parliamentary committee on penal reform. The views of these reformers were taken into account by the authorities; as we have seen, Cold Bath Fields prison contained cells, which the Quaker theorists considered a vast improvement over the cages of the old prisons. They were; no longer did judges and members of the jury catch gaol fever in the court room, and cleanliness became simpler to achieve. But the Quakers considered that solitary confinement in cells was good for the soul, allowing a criminal the opportunity for reflection and considered repentance. This system (known as the 'separate system') was first developed in Philadelphia, and English observers went across the Atlantic to see for themselves: Dickens condemned what he saw, but Lord John Russell ordered such a model prison to be built in England.

This was Pentonville, completed in 1842. The system was that prisoners were kept locked in their cells throughout their sentence; when they were let

Women prisoners in Brixton, 1856

out for exercise they remained isolated or they had to wear masks. Pentonville was considered a great success, and a further fifty-two prisons were quickly built on the same principle, providing 11 000 cells for 'that calm contemplation which brings repentance'. In 1846 the crank was introduced to give prisoners something additional to do—the crank was entirely useless, a heavy handle which had to be turned a particular number of times each day.

Before the building of these new prisons there had been considerable overcrowding in the gaols, and so the hulks of derelict ships along the Thames and waterways had been used to keep many thousands of convicts in cramped and unhealthy misery. They had been intended mainly for men awaiting transportation. The new prisons relieved the situation somewhat and the hulks ceased to be used in 1858. Transportation itself, although it was thought cheaper in the long term than keeping a man in prison, came to an end in 1868, mainly due to opposition from the Australians. This revived some of the overcrowding problems; between 1788 and 1868 the number of convicts transported had been 160 663 (including 23 500 women), and during the 1820s an average of five ships a year had set out loaded with prisoners.

In the earlier years of the nineteenth century there had been other highly popular forms of punishment. Huge crowds used to assemble outside the prisons on 'whipping days' to see criminals stripped to the waist and flogged 'until their backs be bloody'. One of Elizabeth Fry's achievements was that the public flogging of women was abolished in 1817. The pillory afforded a more participatory form of amusement for the public, who sometimes stoned the victims to death. A newspaper report in 1810 described how four men were put in the pillory at Leadenhall. 'Upwards of fifty women were permitted to stand in a ring, who assailed them incessantly with mud, dead cats, rotten eggs, potatoes, buckets of grub and offal and dung which were brought by a number of butchers' men.' These same ladies used stones on the next two victims with such enthusiasm that the pair were dragged away unconscious and blinded for life.

Public executions were the most popular form of entertainment, and in 1800 there were 223 capital offences. On execution days the shops were closed and business ceased so that the people could enjoy the spectacle. Rooms overlooking the place of execution were rented out to the rich, while the mass of the people stood throughout the night in crowds of up to 40 000. The crowd was described by Dickens in a letter which he wrote to the *Daily News* (after watching the execution of Courvoisier in 1840 outside Newgate):

I was, purposely, on the spot, from midnight the night before; and I was a near witness of the whole process of the building of the scaffold, the gathering of the crowd, the gradual swelling of the concourse with the coming-on of the day, the hanging of the man, the cutting of the body down, and the

An execution outside Newgate prison in 1809

The same scene fifty-five years later, this time supervised by the police

removal of it into the prison. From the moment of my arrival, when there
were but a few score boys in the street, and those all young thieves, and all
clustered together behind the barrier nearest to the drop-down to the time
when I saw the body with its dangling head, being carried on a wooden
bier into the gaol—I did not see one token in all the immense crowd; at the
windows, in the streets, on the housetops, anywhere; of any one emotion
suitable to the occasion. No sorrow, no salutary terror, no abhorrence, no
seriousness; nothing but ribaldry, debauchery, levity, drunkenness, and
flaunting vice in fifty other shapes. I should have deemed it impossible that
I could have ever felt any large assemblage of my fellow creatures to be so
odious. I hoped, for an instant, that there was some sense of Death and
Eternity in the cry of 'Hats off!' when the miserable wretch appeared;
but I found next moment that they only raised it as they would at a Play—
to see the Stage the better in the final scene.

It was Sir Robert Peel who, during his period as Home Secretary, reduced
the number of capital offences and did much to humanise the law. And it was
a necessary part of his overall scheme that as the laws became more humane
so their enforcement became more efficient. Hence the introduction of the

Boys in the exercise yard of Tothill Fields prison

New Police. But it followed from these that the gaols would become vastly overcrowded.

In 1861 the number of capital offences was reduced to four—murder, treason, piracy and the destruction of arsenals and shipyards. So conditions *inside* prison did not significantly improve until the end of the century. This was due to the larger prison population, and to the assumption that any further improvements in conditions would serve only to encourage crime.

The last public execution was in 1868, when the Fenian Daniel Barrett was hanged for the bomb outrage in Clerkenwell. In 1877 (103 years after Howard's initial campaign) the State assumed control of all prisons through the Home Office. More than fifty years after the death of Elizabeth Fry there were tentative steps towards some of the reforms she advocated: in 1898 and 1899 the treadwheel and the less productive forms of hard labour (including the crank) were abolished, and a different kind of establishment was created for young offenders at Borstal in Kent.

But the floggings, the rule of silence, the hunger and the lack of sleep, the terror and the destruction of the personality continued behind the prison walls. It was probably a failure in the Victorian imagination that enabled such barbarism to continue into this century. Sir Robert Peel and the proud middle classes were well-intentioned men, but they were conformists to the massive virtues of their society; those who fell victim to the society were liable to be seen with incomprehension, if they were seen at all. A Victorian man was more accustomed to looking up and identifying with his betters; he seldom looked down into the prisons, and when he did he rarely saw a reflection of his own image.

It took such a man as Oscar Wilde, when he came out of Reading gaol, to protest against the treatment of children and lunatics and even prison warders, to mock the idea of inspectors (proposed as a reform) who would ensure that the system worked efficiently when it was the system itself which was at fault. And it took Bernard Shaw to declare to his wide audiences that prison itself was perhaps a worse fate than the stocks, the whipping post or hanging.

This limitation to Victorian reforming zeal was also apparent in the legislation passed by parliament to control the evils of Arnold Pipkin's 'underworld'. The laws in many respects made matters worse—or created new problems.

Off-course cash bookmaking was banned in 1853 and so a whole new area of criminal offence was created where what was needed was control. Legislation against baiting animals, cockfighting and so on, was only introduced when such amusements had almost disappeared. Every kind of prostitution was made illegal in 1885 because venereal disease was such a national problem with the result that control became impossible (an Act in 1864 had provided for inspection of prostitutes thought to be carrying disease).

The Common Lodging House Act of 1851 made lodging houses subject to inspection, required the owners to keep a register and established standards of habitable decency. Local authorities were empowered to close bad lodging houses, but as they were unwilling or unable to provide alternative homes for the very poor the Act resulted in only a marginal improvement. Perhaps the great Victorian principles of self help and charity made it difficult for local authorities to provide the services which they were *empowered* to provide. We have seen that the development of a national police force came slowly, and the same pattern in growth applied to an efficient fire fighting service and improvements in public health, sanitation and safety.

It was the cutting of New Oxford Street through the Holy Land that began the real changes in London, literally opening up such places to daylight. The large building redevelopment which took place in Victorian England did as much to disperse the colonies of crime as railway development did to disperse the footpads and highwaymen, tinkers and tramps. Neither disposed of the causes of crime. These causes were what Christian mission workers were attacking when they went among the poor, providing soup and setting up ideal lodging houses, providing schools and free Bibles. They created some considerable changes among the poor. They also contributed to the change

Street urchins as a phenomenon continued even after the Victorian era. These were photographed in 1888

in the attitudes of society at large, helped by such writers as Dickens and Carlyle who were campaigning for a change of heart.

In 1850 Karl Marx was living in London and working in the British Museum on his massive 'Capital'. He was not concerned with the rookeries or the immediate poverty of his own family but with the manner of an economy which could produce such poverty. His work did not cause any immediate change, and the continuing radical tradition which we have seen represented by the Jacobins and the Chartists was less than effective at the height of Victoria's reign. But as a costermonger said to Mayhew, 'People fancy that when all's quiet that all's stagnating. Propagandism is going on for all that. It's when all's quiet that the seed's a-growing. Republicans and Socialists are pressing their doctrines.'

By the 1890s Bernard Shaw and the Fabians were no longer trying to reform the poor or improve their conditions, they were trying to abolish them. Education was being taken seriously and being put into practice: the London Mechanics' Institute was shortly to become Birkbeck College, and other Mechanics' Institutes all over the country were being turned into technical colleges. The real, underlying questions were being discussed, and the radical tradition was becoming moulded into a political party with members in the House of Commons. Christian mission workers and writers who believed in a change of heart were part of this movement which is now called the Labour Party. It is arguable, however, whether the disappearance of the worst aspects of Victorian poverty were abolished through the flexibility of the political system or the necessities of the First World War.

We have considered prisons and punishments and poverty at such length because they are an inescapable extension of the policeman's role in society. The law defines the social and political boundaries of our behaviour, and it is a policeman's duty to patrol those boundaries. It is for this reason that Sir Richard Mayne's first pronouncement to his force, that a policeman's role is to prevent crime (i.e. to keep people out of trouble), is the only civilised attitude to adopt. .

Appendix 1
Glossary of Cant Words

alderman	half-crown
bearing up	robbery by using a woman accomplice to decoy the victim
bit faker	coiner
bug hunting	robbing drunks
bull	five shillings
cracksman	safebreaker
esclop	policeman
fogle	silk handkerchief
gonoph	petty thief
kingsman	coloured neckerchief
lavendar, in	hiding from the police
lushington	drunkard
nethersken	low lodging houses
pig	policeman or detective
rampsman	footpad ('mugger')
rookeries	slum areas
shoful	counterfeit money
shofulman	a passer of counterfeit money
smasher	a passer of counterfeit money
snide	counterfeit
soft	paper money
steel	prison (after the Bastille in France)
tail	prostitute

Appendix 2
Further Work

There are many different ways in which this material can be followed up. For example, the history of a local police station is bound to prove illuminating. When was it built, and due to what pressures? When was the local police force formed, and why then? In addition to national legislation there are usually local factors, such as a particularly shocking crime or an outbreak of specific lawlessness to stimulate the sudden desire for efficiency. Pupils might be encouraged to use the local archives in their public library to do research on that particular crime and its solution. Local newspapers in Victorian times were filled, as they are now, with accounts of villainy, detection and trial, which can be useful in such research.

Another useful exercise would be to interview a retired policeman; if he joined the force soon after the First World War he is likely to have served under an inspector or superintendent of genuine Victorian vintage. It will be instructive to look into the penal history of the locality, which varied enormously from place to place. Villages will have had their stocks and whipping posts, towns their prisons and houses of correction, coastal areas may have had hulks at some time, and these will all have conformed to the changes which we outlined in 'The National Scene'. If a prison or a gibbet is difficult to locate, examine the street names for an indication. There is no Police Museum open to the public, but many general museums contain something of relevance to our subject—Victorian police uniforms, a selection of bullseye lanterns, material relating to Victorian crime. A visit to such a museum will help to bring the 'peeler' and his period to life.

There are many topics which arise out of this material which could usefully be discussed in class, especially since these topics are so often discussed as though they are new. Law and order, as we have seen, was unenforceable before an efficient police force was created; once we had that efficient police force then the 'bloody code' of savage punishments was moderated and has gradually been replaced by an effort to understand and cure the causes of crime. A class discussion will very quickly settle on the question of whether we have gone too far in moderating those punishments—a question which was already being asked in 1850.

Many of Arnold Pipkin's problems are still police problems today, and a discussion of these will demonstrate one value of history—that it enables us better to understand our contemporary society. In this connection tape recorded interviews by students with modern policemen will be a useful exercise. It will be found that the relationship between the police and the public are still delicate, and that a policeman's duties still include the same wide range of 'extras' such as coping with homelessness, poverty, traffic congestion and political agitation or reform.

Sources for a work on Victorian policemen are limited, except to the extent that they lived in a particular society and dealt with a particular range of problems which are all very well documented indeed. It is perhaps appropriate, therefore, to comment on 'sources' under the section devoted to further work, so that pupils may understand the work methods used for this book

First, I was fortunate enough to be conducted round the Bow Street Museum of Police History by Chief Superintendent John Childs, who also supplied me with a list of official documents to study at the Public Records Office. I had numerous conversations with an ex-inspector of police who has long been retired. Not only the art of the novelist but history as a subject depends to some extent on 'feeling' and understanding of a period so that the facts have a context, and so these personal contacts were vital.

Feeling and understanding, combined with facts, were gained by re-reading Dickens' journalism; Wandsworth libraries contained the complete run of *Household Words*, in which the police and their activities and the conduct of crime were a recurring theme. Henry Mayhew was writing at the same time, and his *London Labour and the London Poor* was essential reading, as was *Criminal Prisons of London and Scenes of Prison Life* which Mayhew wrote with John Binney. Royal Commissions are relentless in their recordings of fact, and there have been many on the police. The two most recent which I used were *The Report of the Royal Commission on Police Powers and Procedure* of 1929 and *The Royal Commission on the Police in 1962*. The standard reference work, which was absolutely invaluable for facts and figures, was Leon Radsiowicz's *History of English Criminal Law and Its Administration from 1750*. In writing about a rather narrow period of time, 4 July 1850, I naturally made extensive use of *The Times*, the *Illustrated London News* and the Annual Register for that year, all of which were in the stock of Haringey libraries.

Appendix 3
Further Reading

Kellow Chesney, *The Victorian Underworld*, Temple Smith, 1970.
Charles Dickens, *Oliver Twist*, Oxford University Press, 1966.
Charles Dickens, *Sketches by Boz*, Oxford University Press, 1957.
Henry Goddard, *Memoirs of a Bow Street Runner*, Museum Press, 1956.
Patrick Pringle, *Hue and Cry*, Museum Press, 1955.
Patrick Pringle, *The Thief Takers*, Museum Press, 1958.
A. A. W. Ramsey, *Sir Robert Peel*, Macmillan, 1971.
D. Rumbelow, *I Spy Blue*, Macmillan, 1971.
Sir Harold Scott, *From Inside Scotland Yard*, André Deutsch, 1963.
Francis Sheppard, *The Infernal Wen*, Secker and Warburg, 1971.

Index